ALBERT EINSTEIN

A COMPLETE BIOGRAPHY

VINOD KUMAR MISHRA

PRABHAT
PRAKASHAN

Published by
PRABHAT PRAKASHAN PVT. LTD.
4/19 Asaf Ali Road,
New Delhi-110 002 (INDIA)
e-mail: prabhatbooks@gmail.com

ISBN 978-93-5521-785-1
ALBERT EINSTEIN: A COMPLETE BIOGRAPHY
by Vinod Kumar Mishra

Edition
First, 2023

Price
₹ 400 (Rupees Four Hundred Only)

Printed at
Sanjay Printers, Sahibabad

Foreword

Good biographies are always a delight to go through and profitable for readers. Therein, authors present, in a few pages, life-time experiences, lessons learnt or dreams experienced. These biographies nourish our feelings and promote our understanding of life.

When I went through the manuscript of this interesting book on Einstein, it whetted my appetite, urging me to read more about him. The result was an admiration for this scientist and philosopher. I regretted not having read earlier in detail about him. Anyone going through this book on Einstein will find this academic exercise richly rewarding. Very few know that this famous Jew was offered the presidency of the newly born state of Israel; he, however, refused. Through this book, Mr Mishra provides the reader with an opportunity to peep into the life of one of the greatest men who lived in the twentieth century, his humble beginnings, his genius and his rise to eminence.

Perhaps Mr Mishra's efforts to present the scientist to his readers, afresh, five decades after his departure from this world, will seem a bit unusual. Just recall that for about 40 years, Harvey, a retired pathologist from Princeton, had been the quixotic custodian of the 20th century's most famous brain. In 1955, he conducted a routine autopsy of Einstein after the 76-year-old physicist had died at Princeton Hospital. The remains were to be cremated. Harvey, however, decided to preserve the organ – his brain – which was responsible for the theory of relativity and the principle for the atomic bomb. Subsequently, efforts were made to study the brain though the mystery behind such intelligence still remains unresolved.

All that goes to show that studying the man is still profitable. It is remarkable that Mr Mishra has taken up as his life's mission the study of extraordinary men who have adorned the pages of history. His earlier work, *Eminent Disabled People of the World,* is an eye opener to the human potential that lies buried in the disabled, whom we look at only with pity. Its reading will make ordinary people sit up and wonder why they are so drab and uninteresting while the blind, the deaf and the lame did so much for humanity.

Einstein's life is reflective of the contradictions in modern life and deserves to be studied today. Born a German, circumstances forced him to accept US citizenship. When he suspected Germany of conducting experiments to perfect the bomb, he alerted the United States to the danger in the larger interest of the human race. He thought nothing of patriotism and nationalism of the German variety that was the rage in those days. Perhaps, he was motivated by the then persecution of the Jews by Hitler and his aides. Though he made no direct contribution to the making of the bomb, yet he felt sorry for his action in prompting the United States to make the bomb. He turned into a campaigner for peace and a world government.

As a man who struggled against the adversity of his life, he has lessons for all of us. It is interesting to note that Albert Einstein and Isaac Newton, the two great scientists, had suffered from some form of autism. Historical figures including Socrates, Charles Darwin and Andy Warhol probably had a form of autism, known as Asperger syndrome. Asperger syndrome is associated with poor social skills and obsession with complex topics such as music. Researchers at Oxford and Cambridge point out that Asperger syndrome provides a plus, *i.e.* it makes people more creative. "People having this syndrome are generally hyper-focused, very persistent workaholics."

In the early stages, his *Theory of Relativity* faced the ridicule of those who were critical of him. Shortly after Albert Einstein had fled from Germany (in 1933), one hundred Nazi professors published a book (*One Hundred Authors against Einstein*) condemning his *Theory of Relativity*. "If I were wrong," Einstein said in his defence, "one professor would have been enough."

It is appropriate that Vinod Mishra, who had suffered from polio at the age of three, should attempt to study the disabled people of the world who earned fame by their contribution to human civilization. In a sense, the work on Einstein can be said to fall in line with that pursuit.

Great humanist as Einstein was, his ideals must still rule conscientious citizens of today. "Every day, I remind myself that my inner and outer life is based on the labours of other men, living and dead, and that I must exert myself in order to give in the same measure as I have received and am still receiving." Such an expression shows his immense humility and sense of gratitude. His simplicity is also widely known as it is reflected in his statement that the 'trite subjects of human efforts, possessions, outward success, luxury have always seemed contemptible' to him. What moved him in life was a passion for truth, compassion for the oppressed and a sense of mystery that underlies creation. "His religion", he said, "consisted in a humble admiration of the inimitable superior spirit who reveals himself in slight details, which we are able to perceive with our frail bodies and feeble minds."

His concern for the human race is reflected in his constant warning that atomic weapons may lead to obliteration of the human race. "I know not with what weapons World War III will be fought, but World War IV will be fought with sticks and stones."

On August 6, 1945, when the first nuclear bomb was dropped on Hiroshima, 2,82,000 Japanese died and tens of thousands were left burnt, maimed and homeless. When Albert Einstein heard the news on the radio, such was his astonishment that he was rendered almost speechless.

How vehemently he spoke against war! The adaptation to warlike aims and activities has corrupted the mentality of man; as a result, intelligent, objective and humane thinking has hardly any effect and is even suspected and persecuted as unpatriotic. "It is my conviction that killing under the cloak of war is nothing but an act of murder," he thundered. All the brutality, heroism and loathsome nonsense that flourished under the guise of patriotism invited only contempt from him. Well, that is his relevance to modern-day politics.

Mishraji did well in choosing Einstein for his subject. We live in times when war-clouds gather all around and it is appropriate to let people read about a campaigner who protested against all belligerence and hatred and warned the world against the dangers of atomic weapons.

At a time when readers' tastes seem to go awry and perverted themes gain popularity, the author has boldly chosen some of the shining stars of history and civilization to dazzle the minds of innumerable readers. May his pen continue to bear fruit and give much needed nourishment to minds hungering for encouragement and ideals!

—M.P.K. Kutty

Author's Note

Born in Germany, Albert Einstein was a theoretical physicist who was conferred the Nobel Prize in Physics in 1921. He devised the general theory of relativity which is one of the two pillars (the other being quantum mechanics) on which modern physics is based. He is known in popular culture for his famous equation E = mc2 which is now believed to be the most famous equation of all time. He was awarded the Nobel Prize for discovering the photoelectric effect which marked a pivotal moment in the development of quantum theory.

He was born in Württemberg, Germany in 1879. A few weeks later his family moved to Munich, where he was enrolled at Luitpold Gymnasium for schooling. Einstein continued his education at Aarau, Switzerland and in 1896 joined Swiss Federal Polytechnic School in Zurich where he was trained to be a teacher in physics and mathematics. After obtaining his diploma in 1901, he found out that there were no teaching jobs available to him, therefore leading him to accept the position of a technical assistant in the Swiss Patent Office. He completed his PhD in 1905. He produced most of his remarkable work while working at the Patent Office. In 1909 he was appointed Professor Extraordinary in Zurich, in 1911 Professor of Theoretical Physics at Prague and in 1914 he was appointed as the Director of Kaiser Wilhelm Physical Institute and Professor at the University of Berlin. He became a German citizen in

1914 and remained in Berlin until 1933. Later he renounced his German citizenship for political reasons and moved to the United States where he was appointed as a Professor of Theoretical Physics at Princeton. He was accorded the American citizenship in 1940 and he retired from his post at Princeton in 1945. Post the Second World War, Einstein was a prominent figure in the World Government Movement. He was offered the Presidency of the State of Israel which he declined. He collaborated with Dr Chaim Weizmann in establishing the Hebrew University of Jerusalem.

In the beginning of his scientific career, Einstein realized the inadequacies in Newtonian mechanics and his theory of relativity emerged out of an attempt to reconcile the laws of mechanics with the laws of the electromagnetic field. He later extended the theory of relativity to gravitational fields and devised the theory of gravitation in 1916 and the same year he published a paper on general relativity. His deliberations on the problems of statistical mechanics and quantum theory led to an explanation of the Brownian movement of molecules and also gave birth to the particle theory of light. In the year 1917, he applied the general theory of relativity to develop large scale structures of the Universe. He is believed to be a powerful influence behind the United States' commissioning of the Manhattan Project to develop nuclear bombs on the eve of the World War II. Though he endorsed the development of such powerful weapons he never was in the favour of using them. Later he signed a petition with the British philosopher Bertrand Russel famously known as the Russel-Einstein Manifesto that highlighted the danger of nuclear weapons. He was affiliated with the Institute of Advanced Study in Princeton until his death in 1955.

Einstein has left mammoth volumes of works comprising some 300 scientific papers and over 150 non-scientific works.

Among his non-scientific works the most notable ones are *About Zionism* (1930), *Why War?* (1933), *My Philosophy* (1934), and *Out of My Later Years* (1950) etc. The present volume of work is an attempt to bring the genius of Einstein to the reach of common readers at the largest scale possible. It offers some of his most important ideas and thoughts put together for the easy perusal of the readers.

❑

Contents

Childhood

On March 14, 1879, the Einstein couple gave birth to their first child who was named Albert. Before they could celebrate his birth, Hermann's small business was shattered. The reason for his failure was his humility and optimism. They were compelled to leave Ulm and move to Munich. There, Hermann started an electrochemical factory with his brother Jacob. Munich was a large city and the capital of Bavaria. The Catholics were in majority and there were many churches in the city.

The river running through the city had seven bridges over it. Prosperous art-galleries were spread all over the city where large-scale trade in art took place. Art traders came there for business from all parts of Europe.

Hermann Einstein bought a small house in Munich. Hermann, Pauline and little Albert started living there. When Albert was two years old, his sister, Maja, was born.

Albert started speaking very late. He could not speak fluently till he was nine. His parents were worried about him. They felt that he would never be normal.

Albert Einstein suffered from dyslexia. In those days, people had very little knowledge about this defect. According to the teachers who taught Albert, he was a very dull child. The Principal of the school also felt the same. Once his father asked the Principal what his child would become in the future. The Principal said bluntly, "Make him whatever; it does not matter because he won't succeed anywhere." Soon Einstein began to think that he was a dullard. But he started to think about unusual subjects. He developed a great interest in space and time.

Albert started going to school at the age of five. He spent the first five years in a Catholic school as the nearest Jewish school was quite far and its fees were high. The religious sentiments of the Einstein family were never too strong. They never thought that studying in a Catholic school would have any adverse effect on Albert. During his days in that school, Albert felt that he was a Jew, alien from the other children. Once the teacher showed students a big nail. He told them when Jesus Christ was crucified, he was pierced with such nails. As soon as the teacher became aware that there was a Jewish child in the class, he stopped. He did not say that the people who crucified Jesus were the Jews. But the atmosphere in the class was uneasy.

At the age of five, Albert got ill and he had to take bed-rest for a long time. To amuse the child, his father gave him a compass. Albert would fix it and rotate it in different ways but the needle of the compass always pointed in the same direction. Albert thought about it a lot. It enhanced his interest. His mind always roamed in space.

At the age of six, Albert learnt to play the violin. Music was an inheritance. So, he did not have any trouble. But Albert always saw music from different angles. He was interested in the mathematical composition of music. He used to get joy of a different kind with the violin. Slowly, the violin became Albert's soul mate.

Albert was also influenced by his uncle, Jacob Einstein. Jacob was an engineer who used to work on sound. He started to teach Albert algebra with his wonderful methods. Jacob told him that, in algebra, people would hunt down animals whose names they did not know. At the beginning they would name them x, y, etc. When they hunted them down, they would know the correct names, meanings. They would write their evaluation in the form of the answer.

In this way, an interesting picture of mathematics began to develop in Albert's mind. He began to understand mathematics in the form of ladders, trains and ships.

Albert was very impressed by his maternal uncle. His maternal uncle, Caesar, visited him regularly. He loved Albert. His presence would change the environment of the house and enhanced the merrymaking. While returning to Germany from Russia, he brought a model of a steam engine with him and gave it to Albert. This further enhanced Albert's imagination. Later, Caesar got married and settled in Antwerp. He was a good businessman and Albert had the opportunity to visit him very often. They would both have intellectual discussions. Despite all these incidents, till the age of ten, Albert was considered dull and an introvert child who had interests in unusual things quite different from other children.

□

Einstein—The Nincompoop

At the age of ten, Albert was sent to Luitpold Gymnasium for his studies. It was just like any ordinary school. The specialty of this school was its strong discipline. The teachers appeared as though they were lieutenants in the army. The children were taught through threat, power and authority.

These types of hard, disciplinary measures usually destroy feelings and qualities like self-confidence, honesty, etc. in children. Albert was also affected. He started to live in fear and suspicion. He even started suspecting the administration.

But one custom was appreciable. Children were inspired to find solutions to their queries. Albert also used to ask different questions, but he found that the environment of the school was not suitable. One of the teachers was more interested in talking about ancient German civilisation. He glorified the Germans very often.

There was another Jewish boy named Max Talmey in the school. Albert was very impressed by him. That boy was studying medical science. Later, Talmey wrote about Albert, 'Albert was a handsome boy and had dark hair.'

Albert discussed topics on physics and mathematics with Talmey. Talmey gave him some books to read. Albert read them with great interest. Once a week, they used to eat together. At that time, Albert used to put all his doubts to him.

Albert also studied books on philosophy. Kant was his favourite philosopher. He studied the theories of Darwin. Since he had already become interested in mathematics, he started looking at the sciences in accordance with mathematics. Soon, he found that it was not possible to formulate mathematical theories for biological activities. Then, he moved his attention towards non-living things. One of the reasons for his changing interest was that he felt that the daily life of living things was simple. He did not notice any complex physics or mathematics in them.

Albert had very little interest in traditional things. Albert not only questioned but found mathematical hypotheses. About philosophical matters, which the ordinary people easily accepted.

Herman Einstein's business once again received a shattering blow. The situation was so bad that they were forced to leave the city. This time, they decided to settle in Milan, on the other side of the Alps. Herman's in-laws came forward to help them. Some people of the Coch family lived in Geneva. So, it was decided that Hermann would conduct his business under them.

In 1894, Hermann went to Milan with his wife and daughter. Albert was sent to a hostel. A distant relative was given the responsibility of looking after him. It was hoped that Albert would get a diploma so that he might get admission to the University. Hermann wanted to make Albert an electrical engineer.

But destiny decided otherwise for Albert. As soon as he was placed away from the family, his activities became strange. The mathematics teacher complained about Albert and wrote in the report that Albert disturbed the studies of the other students by asking unusual questions in class. The doctor who examined him diagnosed that he had suffered a nervous breakdown. He ought to be sent back to his family.

Thus, Albert was sent back to his parents in Milan without acquiring a diploma. There he met many Milanese. They were totally different from the Germans and appeared civilised.

The obstacles in his studies disappeared when Albert started going to the Swiss school in Milan. By that time, he was fifteen years old. His father's financial problems were not yet over. He was also worried about Albert. Once he scolded Albert severely and told him to abstain from unnecessary philosophy and pay attention to the qualifications required to be eligible for admission to the University.

A solution was formulated. The Swiss Federal Polytechnic School in Zurich was considered the best technical school in Europe. A diploma was not necessary to get admission there. One had to just clear the entrance exam. But there was a problem. In 1895, Albert was just sixteen years old. The normal age to get admission to that school was eighteen years. Despite the fact, it was decided that Albert should be sent to that polytechnic.

During his stay at home, Albert regularly analysed the difficult subjects of science. At the very young age of sixteen, he tried to establish links between electricity and magnetism. Albert wanted to get as much information as he could on subjects like space, electricity, magnetism, etc. Regarding this, he wrote a letter to his maternal uncle. He also wrote on subjects like magnetic fields, electromagnetic theory, elasticity, etc.

The thoughts that emerged from the mind of that sixteen-years-old youth were astonishing. No one was able to understand his thoughts during that period. In the midst of those thoughts, Albert realised that his family had great expectations from him. He knew that he could never become an electrical engineer.

□

Education in Zurich

In 1895, Albert reached Zurich, the capital of Switzerland. This city was full of diversities. It is situated on the foothills of the Alps and was influenced by the art and culture of the Middle Ages. It had a beautiful lake which had seen many great personalities like Lenin, Roja Luxemberg, etc.

In his early days, Albert lived with the family of Gustav Mayer. Gustav was an old friend of his father, who had earlier lived in Ulm. Mother Pauline desired that Albert should not waste time. So, she requested the school authorities to consider his exceptional qualities and admit him as soon as possible. She had felt that Albert's studies were affected by the frequent change of locations.

Albert sat for the exam, but was unable to qualify. On enquiry, it was discovered that though Albert had performed extraordinarily in mathematics yet he was very poor in modern languages and life science. Another reason was that Albert had not prepared well for it. Albert determined that the realistic world is not right for him.

It was like forcing a horse to drink water. But Gustav, his father's friend, applied all his efforts. Eventually, it was decided that Albert should be admitted to a school in Aarau so that he might prepare for the polytechnic entrance exam. The school was located 20 miles to the west.

Albert was astonished to see some unusual things over there. In Switzerland, everyone possessed weapons. Every house had guns hanging on the walls. What surprised him was that the people did not have an aggressive mentality like the Germans. The feelings for democracy were strong. Albert had one more advantage. He resided with the family of Mr. Winteler, the Principal of the school where he was to study. Mr. Winteler was a friendly and kind person. He used to have all types of discussions with his fellow teachers and students. With his students and family he would roam the nearby hills. The mode of education in the school was like that of the universities where lectures on different subjects were delivered in different rooms.

The environment was more pleasant and free. Albert who was always silent began to open up. Once while climbing up 8,000 steps of a hill, he slipped. However, his friends saved him. He did not suffer too much injury. During his stay in Aarau, Albert would compare the people there with the Germans. Here people were more peaceful and less greedy. He did not even feel that, being a Jew, he was different from the others.

He could not deny one truth. Since he was born in Germany, he had German citizenship. When he went to Milan, he wanted to relinquish it but was not able to do so. When he came to Switzerland, he loved the place and wanted to settle there. In 1895, during the Christmas holidays, when he went to his parents in Milan, he expressed his deep desire of relinquishing German citizenship and told them that he did not want to be called a German. In 1896, when he returned to Aarau, he sent in an application for Swiss citizenship. He was so anxious about it that he even sent two memoranda.

The strange thing was that he did not have citizenship of any country. However, in those days, citizenship was not a problem.

In the middle of 1896, Albert sat again for the entrance exam of the polytechnic school. That time, he qualified. After the results, he went to Italy to meet with his parents.

On October 29, 1896, Albert returned to Zurich and started his four-year course. There, he found new friends of different social and economic status and different age-groups. Most of his friends were older than him. Some had come from very far-flung areas like Serbia and Hungary. Most of them had struggled a lot to collect money for their further studies.

Initially, Albert had to face various problems, which were petty. He changed his room several times and the places where he ate. Sometimes, he ate in restaurants and sometimes in the cafeteria. Sometimes, he satisfied his hunger with pastries from the bakery and sometimes he took advantage of the kindness of the Swiss landladies.

He used to go on outings during the holidays. He visited several lakes and mountains. He often visited Aarau to meet his sister who was studying there.

Albert was careless about his clothes. His habits were unusual. Whenever he went to meet his old friends, he forgot something or the other at their place. Very often, people complained about him to his father about this habit. His friends often woke up the landlady late at night to return his items, which he had forgotten at their places.

Albert was fond of nature. He was very fond of greenery around the mountains. While in the lake, he would get illusions, and stopped rowing. Many times, the strong breeze would bring him back to his senses. Then, he would start moving the oars.

He had inherited the knowledge of music. Very often, he invited his Swiss friends and their parents to musical evenings. He expected people to pay attention to his music. If he found the audience not paying attention or the ladies knitting, he would immediately stop playing and put the violin back in its case.

He was quite fond of being close to ladies. Many women liked him. Young Albert attracted girls with his soft silky, black hair and glittering eyes. He also attended girls' parties and played violin for them. He also visited their hostels and enjoyed music in their company.

Since his youth, Albert had been inquisitive. He wanted to understand the physical world. He wanted to collect information and analyse it in terms of mathematics. He also wanted to know about the inner world. He was preparing himself to resist the pervading beliefs. But he did not believe in the traditional ways to do this. He did not indulge deeply in the philosophy of anything to analyse it. His four-year course seemed a hindrance to him because he had to spend a lot of time on it.

He developed a desire to become a teacher of mathematical physics. So, he studied more mathematics and natural sciences. Under the guidance of six professors, he studied Calculus, Geometry, Astronomy, Astrophysics, Ballistics and Geology. He also had to study commerce banking, Swiss politics, philosophy and literature. But he gave more attention to mathematics followed by natural science. He assumed Mathematics was a very wide subject and thought that he would spend all his life just studying a single part. He started to analyse the basic principles of physics in accordance with mathematical methods.

He also used to do extensive practical work in the Physics laboratory. His way of experimenting was quite peculiar. Once he injured his hand. He tried to make his special equipment for his experiments. Once he tried to make some equipment for the proper investigation of the rotation of the earth.

As a student, those four years of Einstein's life (1896-1900) were full of incidents. He did not have much trust in the examination system, but he was successful in his last examination. He obtained a graduate degree in 1900. He scored 4.91 points out of 6.00.

□

End of Unemployment

After his graduation, Albert decided to work as a teacher in the Department of Physics in the Polytechnic School. He was even prepared to become a teacher of a lower grade.

But Albert did not get the opportunity. His other friends had joined good trades. Though Albert was disappointed, yet his self-respect was still intact. He did not even want the support of his influential maternal uncle. He wanted to be successful on his own.

Unemployed, he returned to his parents. He wrote a letter to his mathematics teacher in Zurich and requested him to give him a chance to work as his assistant. Moreover, he wrote that he had given more attention to theoretical physics during his studies. It was quite obvious that Albert did not get any response.

Later, Albert returned to Zurich and worked on a temporary basis as a subordinate to his astronomy and astrophysics professor, who had been appointed as director of the Swiss Federal Observatory.

Albert tried his best to get Swiss citizenship. With this thought in mind, he started to save 20 francs each month. One of the reasons was that the people of Switzerland were friendly with one another and respected an individual's private life.

By the end of 1900, Albert had achieved everything necessary to obtain the citizenship; money, eligibility to become a resident and to employment. On October 19, 1899, he sent a formal application to the Swiss officials to obtain citizenship.

He attached his Character Certificate and a paper as proof of his three-year stay in Switzerland. On July 4, 1900, his father also sent a written statement in support of his application. On February 21, 1901, he got his citizenship of Switzerland.

In Switzerland, it was compulsory for every youth to serve in the army. So, in 1901, Albert presented himself to the Swiss army officers. Luckily, the recruiting officers did not find him physically fit. Albert felt very bad and helpless about it. On getting full Swiss citizenship, he had a better chance to get a permanent job. Being a Jew, he had little chance to get a job in Germany.

He developed an attachment to Switzerland. He felt that the people had a more humanitarian attitude. He hated military rule and admired democracy. The people of Switzerland seemed more tolerant. Interference in daily life was negligible. Later, because of these qualities that Switzerland in general had imbibed, most of the rich people in the world, as also some governments, lodged their money in Swiss banks. However, Albert Einstein could not see any hope of a permanent job in the near future. He once visited his parents in Milan. He wrote a letter to a German chemistry scholar who had done research on catalysts. He requested that he should be given a job in his laboratory so that, along with his work, he might continue his studies. But he did not get any reply. On Albert's insistence, his father also sent a letter, but of no avail. Afterwards, Albert wrote a letter to a Dutch physicist. This time, he also sent a reply postcard with it; along with the description of his educational qualifications, he also sent one of his articles. Soon after dispatching the letter, Albert started to dream about working at the University of Holland. But his dream was not fulfilled because the Dutch physicist, Kamerling, did not even send back the reply postcard.

At that time, a change occurred for the good. A technical school in Winterthur required a mathematics teacher for two months. According to the rules, the permanent teacher was required to serve in the army for a particular duration. As soon as Albert Einstein came to know about it, he wrote a letter to one of his old teachers. In that letter, written on May 13, he requested a recommendation from his professor.

This time, he was not disappointed. He was assigned the responsibility to teach mathematics in the school from May 15 to July 15. Nothing of much importance happened during these months. As soon as the permanent professor returned, Albert had to search for another job.

He read in a newspaper that there was a requirement of a teacher in a residential school. The school was situated in a city on the borders of Switzerland. Albert applied for that post and requested one of his old classmates to recommend his name. The recommendation proved effective and Albert got the job, which was again for a short duration.

This job was like any other job. Discipline was very tough and Albert did not like it. After a few months, he was again in search of a job.

During this period of unemployment and petty jobs, Albert Einstein had prepared his thesis on the kinetic theory of gases. He sent it to the University of Zurich for his Ph.D.

In the meantime, he applied for a second-grade post in the Swiss Patent-office. In the application sent on December 11, 1901, he mentioned his educational qualifications and experience which he had acquired doing petty jobs. He also mentioned that though he was the son of German parents, yet he had been staying in Switzerland since the age of 16 years and had Swiss citizenship.

The Swiss Patent-office was established in 1888 and was still working under its first director, Haller. He was an engineer by profession and he was counted among the most successful engineers of that time. He had made great contributions building the railway network in Switzerland from 1870 to 1880. Haller, who built railway tracks on hills, used to run the Patent-office in his own way, but he was also quite friendly.

Albert had to wait for several months before being called for the interview. The interview took two hours, in which information and literature about new patents were put forward. Albert was asked to make suggestions immediately. During the interview, it became evident that Albert's technical knowledge was negligible.

But Haller was impressed by him. Instead of appointing him as a second-grade technical specialist, he appointed Albert as a third-grade technical specialist. His yearly income was fixed at 3,500 francs.

Broadly speaking, the reason for his selection was his knowledge of mathematics and the remarkable latent talent, which Haller recognised in him. During the interview, it also seemed as though Albert was somewhat lazy.

Albert's days of unemployment ended. As soon as he got his appointment letter in June 1902, he began to work on his permanent job.

New City

Now Albert lived in a new city working on a new post. This city was different from Zurich. It had a river flowing in three directions. The effects of technology and industrialisation were limited and people were more interested in the arts. It was also a tourist city.

A room in the rear of an apartment was given to Albert as his residence. At that time, the Swiss Patent-office was located on the upper floor of the Federal Telegraph Office. Albert went to the office for the first time on June 23, 1902.

Albert was appointed on a temporary basis with the condition that he would be made permanent after his work was assessed. It took a long time for Albert to prove his ability. On September 5, 1904, Haller wrote a recommendation letter to the Federal Council stating that Albert was a useful officer. So, his annual income ought to be increased from 3,500 francs to 3,900 francs. But his job category remained the same. According to Haller, Albert was still weak in mechanical engineering.

□

Working in the Patent-office

Albert started analysing patent applications skillfully. Director Haller was quite satisfied with him. During this period, Albert had obtained a Ph.D. from the University of Zurich. Haller had a feeling that Albert would not stay. But he did not want to lose him.

By then, Einstein had earned respect for himself. In 1905, Einstein presented an article of twenty-one pages in which he put forward several new explanations and definitions regarding the measurement of atoms. Professors appreciated his mathematical knowledge.

Einstein looked for better opportunities in the field of teaching. He sent applications to various places and he did not conceal this from his office. By 1906, he had presented three research papers. For one of these, he received the Nobel Prize sixteen years later. One contained the outlines of the principles of relativity which later gave him a special place in history.

He remained simple throughout his life. Initially, he used to live in a small room from where he walked to his office. He had selected friends. As his research papers were coming into the limelight, the number of people jealous of him increased.

To start with, work in the office was limited. Till 1908, only those discoveries got patented which could be produced as a model as it was easy to understand the model. Controversies did not arise about their usage. At that time, patents were normally given for household or other useful objects. This was very easy to assess for a talented person like Einstein. Einstein had to rewrite some patent applications several times on his own in such a way that they could acquire the protection of the law. In the beginning, he used to read only the technical instructions of the people who had applied and had to understand the drawings attached with them.

He sat in the long, narrow room with many other technical officers. There were objects like a camera, a typewriter and other equipment lying here and there.

Einstein took time for his thoughts even then. He could be compared with other learned people of India like Kabir and Ravidas, who used to think about higher knowledge while weaving cloth or mending shoes. During his work at the patents office, he would think deeply about the laws of Nature.

Einstein's every activity was curious. His first research paper brought him respect from all over the world, but it had nothing to do with his world-famous principle of relativity. His first research paper dealt with the force, which binds atoms in fluids. This research paper forced scientists, who till date considered the atomic theory given by Dalton as final, to review their thinking.

At the start of the third decade of his life, Einstein created a stir in the world of scientists. Between 1901 and

1904, five of his research papers were published. His sixth research-paper was publicly released in 1905. On the one hand, the world was very impressed by him, on the other, Einstein was dissatisfied with his own work. This was a curious phenomenon with him. He viewed his first two research papers as attempts by an amateur. However, he thought regularly about their basics. He used to think about the forces which attracted molecules of a gas towards one another. He also tried to imagine the way in which the molecules of liquids and gases moved.

Many young people got attached to Einstein and remained his friends for a long time. He taught Physics as a private tutor and also released an advertisement in the newspaper for this in 1902. He taught several subjects like Science, Grammar, Geometry, etc.

On Sundays, he went for long walks. During his walks to the lake, he had long discussions on scientific subjects with his companion who was also his student. Albert Einstein was 176 centimetres tall. With brown eyes and a prominent nose he began to attract people.

His voice was also very attractive. During group discussions people were left spellbound by his words.

□

First Marriage

In January 1903, Albert Einstein got married to Mileva Maric. Mileva was the daughter of a farmer. It is believed that Albert got engaged to Mileva during his student days. Perhaps, the marriage was delayed because of his father's death in 1902. Albert went to meet his father when he was on his death-bed. When he came back, he married Mileva.

Mileva was not an attractive woman. There was nothing special about her features and face. Many criticisms have been heard about her language and her behaviour. But she had a sweet voice.

People wondered what induced Albert to marry Mileva. There were rumours that Albert's parents were against this marriage. Albert Einstein often quarrelled with Mileva, but he never mentioned it. He preferred to maintain privacy about his personal life. While giving a lecture in New York, he had said: "Even after three hundred years, personal lives should remain a secret."

After marriage, Einstein was relieved of household work and responsibilities. One statement he occasionally made about his wife was that she was always busy with cleaning the dust, dirt and cobwebs.

He never gave any explanation about his marriage. People never got a clear answer from him. But an impression had already gained ground that though the marriage might not have been suitable, yet it benefited him. After marriage, he was totally absorbed in the theories of Physics. Perhaps, he had only a formal association with his family.

Many wedding anniversaries came and went. With each new anniversary his relations with his wife went from bad to worse. Once one of his students came to meet him and noticed that his socks were dirty. He had not even shaved. These incidents were signs of his tense married life.

After marriage, the Einsteins could not go on a honeymoon. Just a small party was given in a local restaurant. Afterwards, the couple started to live in a small apartment. The absent-minded professor, at times, used to forget his keys and sometimes other things here and there.

Only a few days before their first wedding-anniversary on January 6, 1904, Mileva gave birth to their first child Hans Albert.

Generally, Einsten's time between 1903 and 1905 was full of turmoil. During this period, he gave the final touches to his Principles on Relativity.

□

Period of Discovery

In March 1905, Einstein was just twenty-six years old. Many of his research papers were published but he was not able to build a special image of himself. During this time, while giving a lecture at the University of Zurich, he mentioned the work he had done until then. He also presented a summary of his six research papers. After graduation whatever research he did, it was collected in these papers.

Though the research papers contained a lot of hidden knowledge, yet people did not consider his principles seriously. People thought of him more as a person, who wanted to become a professor, but ended up being a clerk in the Patent-office.

There were many reasons behind these misconceptions. People thought that Einstein had nothing to read and nothing to do. He was not associated in any way with any particular university. In the library of the Patent-office, there were several books on engineering, but books related to Physics were negligible. Einstein was able to read only a few German papers related to Physics. He was not even a member of those groups, where high-level, intellectual and scientific discussions took place.

Despite all the things, the principles Einstein had put forward before the world were remarkable. They were on different subjects and people, till then, held different principles. It is quite obvious that it was not easy for people to understand and believe in these new principles.

Let us consider an example. Since ancient times the Greeks had believed that light is an assemblage of very minute particles, which move in straight lines. The particles move at a high speed and get reflected on colliding with a mirror. Newton also agreed to this.

In the seventeenth century, scientists contradicted this notion. They told that light is not an assemblage of particles but they are waves which move continuously. The question arose how waves could move through space, where there is no medium available. Despite the fact, this theory was accepted for about two and a half centuries.

In the later part of the nineteenth century, scientists like Fresnel and Maxwell made a thorough research on light. An intense discussion on the nature of light got under way. Many theories were put forward but the mathematical equations based on these theories did not prove true in practical results. By then, apart from visible light, other different types of radiations, like X-rays, gamma rays, infra-red rays, etc. were discovered. J.J. Thomson had even identified the electron.

Einstein advanced his new theory that light moved in the form of photon clusters. He gave a mathematical equation for it '$h\nu$ = Energy' where 'h' is Constant which later came to be known as Planck's constant and ν is the frequency of light.

This theory created a stir among scientists. Senior scientists like Planck refused to accept this new theory.

Einstein's other theories were also revolutionary. His theories on the movement of atoms astonished scientists who openly expressed their thoughts about it. Einstein then brought out his remarkable Theory of Relativity.

In the summer of 1905, Einstein presented the outline of this theory. It is still considered the most revolutionary theory. Before this, Newton's theory of gravitation and Charles Darwin's 'origin of the species' were considered to be the most revolutionary theories. Many stories are associated with them, like an apple falling on Newton's head, etc. They also gave a basis for the establishment and development of science.

□

The Joy of Success

At the age of twenty-six in 1905, his five research papers proved that he had exceptional hidden talent and he entered the world of international science.

The editor of the paper, which published the research papers, was very impressed by Einstein. When a professor from Poland read the papers, he was so impressed that he declared Einstein as the second Copernicus. Afterwards, Albert's associates started to increase.

People started to accept his principles of relativity. These principles started to influence the world of science in the same way as when rainwater falls on limestone, most of the water evaporates and only some wets the stone. On the one hand, some people challenged his theories and some totally disapproved of them. On the other hand, many scientists did practical research work based on this and compared the results obtained from practical research with those obtained theoretically. The results obtained from Einstein's formula did not match the results obtained practically. This gave rise to controversy. Technology, at that time, was not advanced enough to execute these types of experiments accurately. So, a peculiar situation arose and no one was in a position to prove that the other was wrong.

People wanted answers to these questions from Einstein. Different letters were sent to him and one such letter came to his patent office in the year 1906. The sender expressed his desire to meet him. That sender, Laue, later met him and spent around two hours with him. They had an intensive and serious discussion.

The discussion was so intense that they did not even realise they had reached Einstein's house as they walked from the office. Laue smoked a cigar Einstein gave him. He did not like the taste but said nothing. This shows how eager people were to learn more about the Theory of Relativity. During this period, people were trying to understand the world with the help of this principle. Many students used to mention this principle in their research papers and books. Often, the examiners did not agree with what was written but they were also unable to reject it. So, they advised the students to talk directly to Einstein on this subject. Many letters came to him regarding the principles and the students also came to meet him directly. In 1907, something like this happened with a student named Lamb. When he came to meet Einstein, the discussion did not last for days but continued for several weeks. Out of these discussions, three combined research works based on electro-magnetism evolved, which are known as the combined achievement of Lamb and Einstein. People were surprised to see how this petty officer of the Patent-office had such enormous knowledge on so many subjects.

Lamb benefited from the combined work with Einstein and got a chance to work as Leonard's assistant. Lamb and Einstein continued corresponding with each other. When

Lamb expressed his disappointment and problems about Leonard's way of working, Einstein suggested to him to be patient and told that working with Leonard would bring him fame and money because Leonard had done the basic work. But Lamb could not continue for long.

When Einstein first wanted to start teaching, no one had given him a chance. But in 1907, Professor Kleiner expressed his desire to have him as his assistant. At that time, the tradition of appointing someone as a professor without teaching experience was not prevalent.

We can guess by this fact that Klainer was so eager to keep Einstein with him that he invited Einstein to take up a post in Bern University. He could serve there and fulfill his responsibilities to the Patent-office at the same time.

Einstein was also eager to join the teaching profession. He applied for a post in the Department of Theoretical Physics. With the application, he attached copies of his research work. He also claimed that he would create such interest in students for physics that his one lecture would be equivalent to two lectures given by anyone else.

Nothing can be gained before time and against the wishes of destiny. Einstein's application was rejected. Many reasons were given. Finally in 1908-09, Einstein got a chance to teach the principles of radiation at Bern University. The first batch had just four students and the next had just a single student. Einstein used to teach this single student in his room. Overall, his teaching was a flop.

But his research work continued during this period. He got a chance to do research work with Herman Minkowski who was born in Russia and once had taught Albert. At that time, Albert seemed a very lazy student to him who did not put in any effort in mathematics.

Minkowski was well versed in mathematics. He prepared several mathematical equations and strengthened Einstein's principle of relativity. Their association could have continued further. But at the end of 1908, Minkowski became ill and on January 12, 1909, at the age of forty-four, he died. He regretted that he had to leave the world before the principle of relativity was finalised.

The year 1909 was auspicious for Einstein. He was invited to Geneva where the 350th anniversary of its establishment was being celebrated. A proposal was made to present an honorary doctorate to Einstein.

Einstein went to Geneva in July 1909, where he was honoured along with Madam Curie. Wilhelm Ostwald was also among the other honoured people who, some years later, were honoured with the Nobel Prize for Chemistry. He had done a remarkable work on catalysts.

He was successful throughout the year. After Einstein returned from Geneva as a physicist, Rudolf Handenbury came to meet him from Berlin. After discussions, it was decided that Albert Einstein would go to Salzburg to deliver his lectures in September 1909.

At Salzburg, he got a chance to speak in front of great scholars like Planck, Wien Rubens and Sommerfeld. He impressed those scholars by whom in turn he had been impressed for long. Einstein had shed his image of a dullard before his thirtieth birthday. He created a stir among scientists of the world with his activities. After giving his lecture in Salzburg, Einstein enjoyed a holiday at a lovely place nearby and returned to Bern. This short recess affected him. He decided that he would quit his job at the Patent-office and become a full-time teacher.

In 1908, a post was created in the Physics Department of the University of Zurich. Professor Klainer had made up his mind to appoint Einstein in this department but it was not so easy for Einstein to teach in his own institute, from where he had graduated.

At that time, another event took place. There was a classmate of Einstein, Fredrick Adler, whose father, Victor, had started the Socialist Democratic Party in Austria. To prevent his son from entering politics, Victor sent him to Switzerland to study physics. But politics accompanied him there. Most of the board members of the University of Zurich were socialists. This affected the selection and the newly created post was given to Addler.

Einstein was not upset about this. Adler thought if the post was offered to Einstein, he would accept it. In very clear words, he said to the board, "This University requires people like Einstein. A person like me is not a patch on Einstein. If Einstein joins, then the level of this University will increase to a great extent."

Adler sent a similar letter to his father in Vienna. On November 28, he requested Klainer to appoint Einstein.

Einstein was looking for other jobs in the field of teaching. He re-applied to a Technical College for a job. At one place, he offered to teach mathematics. He wrote about all this to his friend, Lamb.

Adler's integrity showed results. In early 1909, Klainer called Einstein to Zurich. Though obstacles were still there, yet the chance of an appointment was strong. Einstein's name did not figure in the first list of appointments, which was issued in April.

Slowly, the cloud of uncertainty was removed. Eventually, Einstein made his full-time entry into the field of teaching.

On July 6, 1909, Einstein sent his resignation to the Department of Justice (under which the Patent-office was operating) of the Swiss Government. It was a great setback to the director, Haller, who had all along been very impressed by Einstein. First, he refused to accept his resignation. When he felt that Albert Einstein really wanted to leave, he wrote with a sorrowful heart that his departure would be a great loss to the department. Since Einstein was interested in teaching and scientific research only, he did not think it logical or appropriate to stop him.

Till then, Dr. Albert Einstein had just achieved the rank of an associate professor. His annual income was just 4,500 francs. This salary was not enough to live on in an expensive city like Zurich.

Einstein's desire to join the teaching profession was so keen that he came to Zurich in October 1909. The joy of coming was so intense that he even forgot to inform the police and district officer about his change of residence. The information was sent two days later.

□

A New Path Towards Success

In Zurich, Albert Einstein lived in an apartment with his wife and child. In July 1910, his second child, Edward, was born. That year, he got an increment of a thousand francs in his annual salary. It was given to him as lectureship fees.

Fortunately, Frederick Adler also lived in that apartment block and he had a very good relationship with Einstein. They occasionally met each other. As a teacher, Einstein was quite popular. His way of teaching was innovative. While teaching his students, he used to narrate incidents from his school days and mentioned some other incidents from Munich days.

He gave lectures on subjects like quantum theory, thermodynamics, kinetic theory of gases, electricity, magnetism, etc. In the end, he used only clear and precise words. He used written notes less frequently. The jokes were often related to the subject. He gave all his spare time to the students. After lectures, when he saw his students were tension-free and happy, it gave him eternal pleasure.

Before presenting complicated mathematical equations, he spoke about them jokingly. He was friendly with the students and often had tea with them at the cafeteria. It was not a normal practice at that time. During tea, he discussed important matters about the universe.

When Einstein came to Switzerland, he was just sixteen-and-a-half-years old. He had been living in Switzerland for fifteen years when he came to the University of Zurich. This country seemed paradise to him.

His personal requirements were a pen, a pencil, a sheet of paper, a violin and the lake, where he used to boat. These were the facilities he had in Switzerland. He expected and wanted nothing more.

In the beginning of 1911, a rumour spread in the University that Einstein was leaving for Prague. Everyone was upset. Switzerland had great expectations from him. Frederick Adler, who, for Einstein, had let his opportunity to teach in the same position go by, was also upset. He was on some other post in the same University. He wrote a letter to his father regarding this.

Einstein did not comment at first. Only after a month, he broke his silence that the German University in Prague had asked for his services. Einstein had a desire in his mind to go there but the reasons for it were strange. He said that the city of Prague was very beautiful. There were big palaces, majestic royal decorated churches. In addition, the city was associated with Tycho Brahe with whom Kepler had worked and then made the world understand the rules of the movement of the celestial bodies and other distinguished astronomers.

Perhaps, Einstein wasn't aware of the fact that there was a conflict between the people of Prague and the German rule. There were two universities over there, one was called the German University and the other Czech. Both were established in 1888. The Jews were in a majority in the city and had a great influence over its politics.

Two names had been recommended for the post in Prague. Finally, the Education Ministry chose Einstein. The main reason was that the scholars there felt that if the Theory of Relativity proved to be true, then Einstein would be the second Copernicus. Apart from this, the authorities had slowly and slowly come round to regard his research papers more seriously.

When it was known that the post had been offered to Einstein, the other candidate, Jaomon, said that he had no problem if Einstein was the first choice. Thus, the path for Einstein was clear.

However, a new obstacle appeared. The king had the veto power regarding appointments at the University. He would give the final assent only after the consent of the Church. Though Einstein was a Jew, yet he never went to any place of worship nor did he believe in God.

Thus Einstein lost the race. He also became upset. The main reason was that he felt this would affect appointments in the future. One more reason was that, in Zurich, he was still an associate professor and his salary was very low as compared to what was offered in Prague. In Zurich, he studied under the light of a lantern. In Prague, electricity had been introduced.

Luck favoured Einstein. After talks with the Education Department of Prague in March, 1911, he got appointed. There, he had better facilities. After increase in his salary, for the first time he became mindful of household work and employed a maid servant. Ludwig, his assistant, helped him a lot in this regard.

He also noticed some capriciousness there. The population of the Jews was very large but they were divided among themselves. Slowly, he became friendly with many people. One strange thing was that he was a German by birth. He had given up German citizenship by his own free will. Again, he had returned to teach in a German University. Though he did not like it, yet he was aware that he was being pressurised to take up Austro Hungarian citizenship. This problem was more complicated for him than any of his problems related to physics. In the meantime, by his own will he became a member of the Jewish community over there.

Among his friends, Franz Kafka, Hugo Burgman, Max Brod, etc. are worth mentioning. All of them frequently gathered at the residence of Bartha Fanta. He had many artists and scholars as friends. Some people were also trying to unite the Jewish community over there.

Einstein started further research on the work of Tycho Brahe and Kepler. He discovered that Kepler never did research with a fixed aim. Many different thoughts disturbed his mind but he was farsighted. Einstein was very impressed with Kepler's ways.

Einstein now started to consider himself a Jew. This may have been the effect of his Jewish friends on him. He collected detailed information about the history of the Jews and studied the achievements of famous Jews in different fields.

During his stay in Prague, Einstein continued his research on magnetism. Since he had become more popular, he received invitations to give lectures at many different places. From October 30, to November 3, 1911, he gave lectures at the Congress session held in Brussels. It was organised by a chemistry scholar in Belgium. His name was Ernest Solvay. He was motivated by Walther Nernst, a very popular German. Solvay had patented his processing of soda. Many companies were using his method and supplying soda to the world. He wanted to spend a part of his acquired wealth for the development of science.

Many well-known scientists presented their research papers at the Congress. Einstein not only presented his paper but also held discussions with scholars like Planck, Nernst, Lawrence, etc. He met Madame Curie, who was at the height of her popularity at that time. He also met Ernest Rutherford. Einstein for his calculations and Rutherford for his experiments got special praise. He met Lindemann also, who was just twenty-five years at that time and later earned a reputation by doing war-related scientific work for Britain during the Second World War.

Detailed discussions were held on radiation and quantum. Einstein discussed special heat-related discrepancies at room temperature. Madame Curie appreciated Einstein's clear views and his way of presentation. Other scientists participating in the Congress had similar views.

Einstein now thought about leaving Prague. One reason was Mileva. Mileva played an important role in his leaving Switzerland. She started something of this sort in Prague also. She was unhappy living in Prague. Though she was Yugoslavian, she went to Switzerland for her studies. She was an unstable woman. Because of her mercurial nature, her mind did not stick to one particular place.

Initially, Einstein did not pay much attention to the matter. He had become quite fond of the library in Prague. By that time, a post of a mathematics professor had become vacant in his old institute, ETH, in Switzerland.

Now Einstein had a long list of people who would recommend his name. From Paris, Madame Curie wrote a letter in his favour. Many renowned scientists also wrote letters. Einstein himself also wanted to teach where he had studied.

At last, in August 1912, he returned to Switzerland. He was appointed for ten years at ETH. This time, he selected a new residence in Zurich. Altogether, it was his fifth residence over there.

By the end of 1912, Einstein had started organising a seminar every weekend wherein he revealed his new research works. Not only was the environment of this teaching institute familiar to him, Einstein had also achieved a strong position there. The professors and the students of the institute as well as of distant universities came to him. So many people used to gather there that there was not enough place to accommodate them.

But Einstein delivered his lectures without being affected. Many eager people used to ask him questions and surround him. Many students would note down the answers in their notebooks. Often in winter, the snow would fall on the notebooks of the students. Their efforts to remove snow would be an exercise in futility. This did not upset Einstein or his students or his audience.

Many great scholars visited Einstein frequently. Madame Curie came to him along with both her daughters. She was well versed in both physics and chemistry. Einstein had long discussions with her on radioactivity.

Einstein also used to have serious discussions with the professors of engineering. Einstein's father had wanted him to be an engineer, but he could not fulfill his father's desire. Slowly, Einstein started taking an interest in philosophy and his lectures contained some philosophical thoughts. He began to think about the whole universe. His theory of relativity was becoming mature. He was frequently involved in connecting his theories with theories propounded by other scholars.

This was the era when scientists like Niels Bohr, Planck and Rutherford were introducing various new theories in Physics. These people were observing the atom and its various possibilities from different angles. These scientists would discuss the problems they perceived sitting together and carried forward their work. They were from different countries and the politicians of Europe were preparing for war, yet these scientists were in a world of their own and unaware of the political animosity raging around them. Nobel Prizes for various disciplines had been introduced in 1901. Not that people had not taken note of these prizes. Over time, their importance had also increased manifold. Despite the political climate, there was no rivalry among the scientists.

Einstein wanted to verify his Theory of Relativity practically. For this, in 1914, he was waiting for the solar eclipse which was likely to occur in that summer. It was decided that it should be observed from some suitable place in the south of Russia. For this, a team was created. It comprised of famous geologists. At that time, Germany was preparing for war and the officers in Berlin were not at all interested in this type of experiment on theoretical physics. But they gave permission to the team of scientists to go to Russia at their own expense.

Many efforts were made to collect money. It was not easy for a poor scientist to collect such a huge amount. Suddenly, the Germans began to take interest in the mission. Perhaps, they saw potential in Einstein. He was offered a job in Berlin. The officers in Berlin felt that Dr. Einstein was a German by origin. So, it would be better to keep him in Germany. They offered to almost double his salary.

On December 7, 1913, Einstein accepted the proposal of doing research in Germany. On April 6, 1914, Einstein with his wife Mileva and their two sons went to Berlin. What a wheel of fortune! Einstein who was born in Germany and relinquished its citizenship seventeen years ago by his own will, saw the probability of a future in the same environment, which he hated when he was young. The question of citizenship came up again. But he had become a member of the Prussian Science Academy. Through it, he had the citizenship of Prussia. Einstein did not want to relinquish his Swiss citizenship but he was bound to accept the German one. In the meantime, a new law was formulated in Germany according to which any foreigner selected for a government job automatically gained German citizenship.

After coming to Berlin, Einstein started living in a rented flat. On July 20, 1914, he delivered his first lecture at the Academy. Every day in the morning, he went to the office of the Academy which was situated in a government library. When the office asked about his work-related requirements, he just asked for paper and pencil. Along with it, he desired time for thinking and he also told them that he didn't want to interfere in other people's work.

Until then, he had been attempting to analyse science and philosophy. He saw that, in scientific research, the interference of politics and power had increased considerably. At that time, the political situation of Europe was disturbed. War clouds were hovering over the Continent. People were longing for peace. Einstein was also among them.

The atmosphere in the Einstein family was deteriorating every day. Mileva had been a complaining type right from the very beginning. When Einstein was in Switzerland, Mileva used to get irritated with his friends. In 1914, Mileva along with her two sons went back to Switzerland.

In August 1914, Germany declared war against Russia. Two days later, Germany declared war against France also. As soon as the German Army entered Belgium, Britain declared war against Germany on August 4.

Einstein's dream to visit Russia in order to prove the reliability of his theories fell through on account of war. Those scientists who had already gone to Russia for the initial preparations were arrested and their appliances were seized. Scientists, who went to see the solar eclipse, were put into prison.

They were released after long discussions with senior Russian officers. They returned on September 2. They were from different places but they were trapped in Berlin during the World War. For a short duration, they were employed in temporary jobs in the observatory there. They helped Einstein in his research work. Einstein's plan to prove the reliability of his theory was ruined.

In the wake of war, Mileva continued to live in Switzerland with her children while Einstein stayed in Berlin. Perhaps, both did not care much about each other. Einstein spent his holidays with his friends from academic world. He even celebrated Christmas with his fellow professors. Now the violin was his only soul mate. Einstein's friends were sympathetic about his family situation. But they had also realised that, with his family away, Einstein was able to do his research work in a better way.

Einstein was quite fond of both his sons. He remembered them a lot on Christmas eve in 1914. At that time, his elder son was ten years old and the younger was four years old. He did not want the situation in the world and the family to affect the upbringing of his children. By that time communication links between Germany and Switzerland were broken.

Altogether, World War I influenced Einstein a lot. It affected his scientific thoughts. His family conditions worsened. He thought that his scientific work must be kept away from the government. Intelligence and loyalty were enough. During the war, he noticed a totally different situation.

Anyway, scientists can remain away neither from society nor from power. Newton was chief advisor to the British Admiralty. Scientists like Michael Faraday, Dewar, etc. could not abstain from political or social activities. Politicians had used dynamite, which was invented by Alfred Nobel.

Einstein's subject was theoretical physics. He thought he could keep away from politics and political power. He was not bothered by the fact that Hauf who had held the post before him, which he had now, was involved in preparing arms and armaments for Germany. His old assistant, Ludwig, was involved in research to prepare fighter planes. Many of his friends and acquaintances or assistants were involved in war-related works. Some were serving the military and some the air force. One of Einstein's students was doing war-related mathematical calculations on the eastern front for the army. Chemical scientists were preparing chemicals for the bomb and the geologists were collecting various data.

Any scientist is, first of all, the citizen of his country. He has the same patriotism as any other people. This was the reason why the scientist, Fritz Haber, became very upset and a victim of severe depression when he was denied admission to the army because of his physical condition. Later, when the army required gasoline which could work at low temperatures, because they had to fight on the Russian battle front in the snow, Haber was called. On hearing the demand, his depression disappeared. He became happy.

In the uniform of the German Army, he went up to his wife and said, "I am a scientist for the whole world during peace, but at the time of war, I belong to my country."

Haber created a revolutionary technique to prepare ammonia. With its help, it became easy to store explosive and catalytic products. This technique proved very helpful for the Germans during the war. Though he was a professor and he received the Nobel Prize, yet he was given the rank of Captain. He not only did research for the army, but he also inspired other scientists to do so. When research on gas masks started, he inspired his assistant scientists and gave them the rank of Sergeant. Haber had also worked with the team which created chlorinated gas for the German Army. In 1917, Haber gave a gift to the German Army in the form of mustard gas.

Einstein was in a dilemma in this environment where his fellow scientists showed patriotism. Though he was born in Germany, he had not much attachment to the land and conditions there. He saw that in the situation of war, the scientists and common people all spoke the same language in favour of the country. Their old professional rivalries were forgotten.

He was looking for the scientists who protested against the war or, at least, were indifferent to it. He came to know Madame Curie was driving ambulances and was taking care of wounded soldiers. This gave him some satisfaction. Einstein, who had dreamt of becoming a scientist since his childhood and who had struggled a lot to achieve the position of a scientist, started getting very depressed. He knew that Germany was very aggressive but the alliance nations were no less. Both sides had made science a prostitute of war.

While the entire scientific world was showing patriotism by their services for the war, Einstein was looking towards globalisation and socialism. At that time, he had no regard for what the people in top authority were demanding.

Despite being acquainted with the thoughts of Einstein, many of his scientist friends tried to pull him towards service for war. Leopold Copel also offered a grant to him for war-related research, but these efforts were not enough to move Einstein. He continued regarding Germany as aggressive. Thoughts against war had made a deep impact on his mind. He was not in agreement with those scientists who believed that if Germany had not started the war, German traditions would have been totally eliminated from the world.

Einstein was also struggling on another front. His wife was far away in Switzerland. His only contact with her was through letters. Einstein started to feel that he would emerge a loser in his family life. Even then, he put in every effort to gain public opinion against the blood-bath occurring in Europe.

On August 19, 1914, he sent two letters to two scientists living in Holland i.e. Eliren-fest and Lorentz. In the letters, he criticised the naked dance of inhumanity occurring in Europe. It was evident that despite several setbacks in his efforts for world peace, he would continue trying.

On November 16, 1914, Einstein became a member of a political group, whose aim was to establish peace. One of its founder members, Hugo Simon, became a minister after the war. The aim of these people was to create such a situation that the probability of war did not arise again. Einstein was more vociferous than other members of this group. He opined that peace must be established at any cost even if in the process of doing so, Germany faced defeat.

When Einstein heard about the peace efforts by the famous writer and philosopher, Romain Rolland, he wrote a letter to him in March 1915. In September 1915, he crossed the German border and went to meet him. Rolland was very impressed by Einstein and he wrote about him in detail in his diary.

Einstein's campaigns against war were welcomed in Switzerland. By now, people knew that the Jews were found all over the world. They did not remain attached to any particular country. That was why in such a critical situation, Einstein was talking vociferously about world peace.

There were various other reasons why Einstein protested against the war. He was upset that his friends like Haber were involved in the preparation of destructive poisonous gases.

When Germany challenged America over the U-Boat, Einstein became more worried and he felt that now the war would spread further and become more violent.

Einstein was still a Swiss citizen. On this count, he had the freedom to travel to neutral countries. Taking advantage of this during Easter of 1916, he visited his wife in Zurich.

In 1916, he went to Holland on an official invitation by Lorentz. As they were smoking their cigars, Einstein and Lorentz had a long discussion over the bending of light in a magnetic field. Lorentz asked several questions on this subject and Einstein kept giving the answers. He gave some answers very easily, but found some difficult. In between, he also noted some points and mathematical formulae.

When Einstein returned, he met his old friend Adler, who was, like him, against the war. Adler had left Switzerland in 1912 and had gone to Austria. He had been quite interested in politics since early times. When the government there refused to call the session of parliament, Adler became very angry and he shot the Prime Minister dead in a hotel.

Adler was convicted of murder and a law suit was filed against him. During this period, he was imprisoned. During his stay in prison, Adler wrote a book on Einstein's Theory of Relativity. This theory and the research book on the Theory of Relativity were used in the court to prove that Adler had really become mad. So, he should not be punished.

The death sentence was announced for Adler. Due to some reason, his punishment was remitted. Finally, he was sentenced to just eight months of imprisonment. This was the minimum punishment for the murder of a prime minister.

Adler was kept as a prisoner in a fort where he continued his scientific study. His contacts with Einstein through letters continued till the end.

□

Period of Hardship

Between scientific development and protests against the war, Einstein had to face a period of hardship. His family was about to split. During Easter of 1916, Einstein went to meet Mileva; the tension between them had reached its peak. An intense quarrel occurred between the two. A decision was taken that they would not see each other again.

Tension between them continued even after the above quarrel. Albert Einstein's son Hans also stopped writing to his father. In between, he got the news that Mileva was sick. Einstein was not able to build enough courage to meet her, even though he felt that his son would think his father did not care. Different thoughts started to haunt his mind. He unburdened himself in his letters to his friend Besso.

As a result of all these hardships, Albert Einstein himself became the victim of a nervous breakdown. He also developed a terrible infection. It could have been because of the lonely life that he was living. There could have been some carelessness with regard to food.

One of his friends took him for a check-up to an acquaintance's wife who was a doctor. After thorough investigation, it was proved that he was not a victim of cancer. The disease in the stomach had taken quite a severe form. The doctor was also of the view that Einstein had used his brain beyond its limits for scientific work, especially for the development of the theory of relativity. The terror of war also affected his heart and mind very deeply and all these had directly affected his stomach.

Einstein began to behave in a strange manner. He thought deeply about the universe and his mind explored beyond boundary. Now his body had also ceased to follow any boundaries. He would sleep until someone woke him up. He remained awake until someone made him sleep. He remained hungry until he was given food. When he was given food, he continued eating until he was stopped.

While Germany was losing on the battlefront, Einstein was losing his health. Just in two months Einstein had lost twenty-three to twenty-four kilograms of his weight. All his movements had become haphazard. During the war, chaos prevailed everywhere. Still, many of Einstein's friends helped him. Many people kept visiting him. One of his female friends, who had come to see him, asked him once if he feared death. Einstein answered in a philosophical way, "I consider myself as a part of everyone. I am just a minor part of mankind, whose extinction I don't fear."

Even in such a state, Einstein wrote one or two letters and his friends were astonished to see that he was not at all worried about his wife and children. Einstein still had to face one more blow. His mother had come to Berlin to spend her last few months with him. When she died, Einstein wept bitterly. People were astonished to see him, because they thought that Einstein did not have much interest in worldly matters and he was only dedicated to science. Perhaps, that was for the better. It relaxed his mind, which had been suffering from the burden of science and the war.

There was also a good side to this disease. He had a cousin, Elsa, who was a mother of two daughters. She was beautiful and attractive. Unfortunately, Elsa became a widow when she was very young.

There was a considerable difference between Elsa and Mileva. She was inquisitive and wanted to know things. On the other hand, Elsa was very simple and had little knowledge. Her desires were also limited, but she was quite adept at household work.

Einstein had totally involved himself in science, politics and peace efforts. Elsa had nothing to do with these things. During his illness, she took care of Einstein.

In 1917, after his illness, Einstein went to Switzerland. Away from the war, he felt a peculiar peace over there.

Einstein had not met Mileva since 1916, but he continued to fulfill his responsibility towards his family. He received an annual salary of 13,000 marks and he sent 7,000 marks to his wife and children. Till his mother was alive, he used to send her 600 marks. He was not able to maintain the standard of living of a professor on the remaining money. He managed his livelihood with considerable difficulty.

As the war came to an end so too did Einstein's married life. In the summer of 1918, Einstein sent a message through Besso that if Mileva was ready for a divorce, he would continue paying for the expenses of Mileva and the children. During that time, a rumour started spreading that Einstein was to be awarded the Nobel Prize. It was almost decided that from the interest of the prize, which was 30,000 Kroner, the family expenditure could be managed.

In July 1918, the divorce papers were prepared. Albert and Mileva produced themselves before the court in Berlin. At the same time, Einstein discovered through some of his Dutch friends that a group of Dutch scientists were going to do a practical test on his theory on the day of the next solar eclipse, which was in 1919. That period was full of incidents and news. After the US had joined the war, the alliance nations became stronger. For the first time in four years, the position of the Germans on the west front was weakened. Britain had gained a decisive victory over Germany's ally Turkey. Also, power in Germany had changed hands. Internal law and order had deteriorated.

Einstein's scientist friends who were involved with war-related scientific work returned one after the other. Many were compelled to work on meagre wages in their posts. On the other hand, Einstein's popularity was spreading to distant places. Along with Eddington, all the British scientists were preparing to test Einstein's Theory of Relativity in practice on the day of the forthcoming solar eclipse on May 29, 1919. Einstein's hypothesis about the universe was being studied in scientific institutions all over the world. An intense debate over the origin of the universe, its development and future had started in earnest.

□

After Germany's First Defeat

Einstein was a man of the world. He was born in Germany. Irrespective of what country he belonged to, he would get involved in discussing world peace whenever he got a chance.

During the First World War, with the exception of a few people like Einstein, all of Germany was ready to die for the country and they were happily bearing the hardships that arose due to the war. During the war, Germany inflicted atrocities at many places, but the German citizens did not consider it as tyranny.

After their defeat, Germany faced a famine in 1919. Einstein who sympathised with the Alliance Nations during the war was upset. He felt that in the madness of victory, the Alliance Nations had also behaved in the same way.

At the end of 1919, Einstein got a chance to visit Zurich, where he gave a lecture at the University and at ETH. In January 1919, he returned to Berlin.

In February 1919, Einstein got his divorce from Mileva. Einstein had already promised that when he would get the

Nobel Prize money, he would give it to Mileva. He received the Nobel Prize after three years and the prize money came from Sweden to Berlin and thereafter to Zurich. Owing to the foreign money regulations and mismanagement, a lot of money was lost and Mileva got the leftover money in the form of a magnificent house in Zurich.

Another peculiarity was that the couple fought with each other as long as they lived together. When they were separated, the bitterness between them vanished. After the divorce, Mileva continued to call herself Mileva Einstein. She suggested that Albert should go in for a second marriage. She knew about Albert's relations with Elsa.

After the divorce, Mileva lived for almost tweny-five years. She was ill most of the time and also faced problems with her youngest son.

On June 2, 1919, Albert Einstein got married to Elsa. After getting married in Berlin, the couple went to Zurich. There, they discussed the future plans for both the children with Mileva. On June 25, they came to Berlin. On June 28, they returned to Switzerland, where they stayed for three months. On September 21, 1919, they returned to Berlin.

When Einstein returned to Germany, the Jewish movement was spreading its wings throughout Germany. A team of Jews met him and forced Albert Einstein to realise that he was a Jew.

Discussions about the German tyranny in Belgium and France during the war were also quite prevalent. Einstein had very little knowledge about international politics. Sometimes, he made comments which hurt the Germans.

After the war, Albert Einstein distributed his time equally between scientific and non-scientific work. He openly participated in scientific seminars and people started to understand his theories on light, magnetism, relativity, etc.

When he gave lectures, people listened to him with keen interest and concentration. But he was utterly confused regarding politics. He himself did not know in whose favour he was. The behaviour of the Alliance was the same as the Germans after their victory. German scholars were boycotted. Protests were raised against inviting scholars like Heisenberg, Max Born, Planck and Einstein to seminars. Others remarked that without them the seminars on physics would be useless. It was hoped that with the passage of time the bitterness would diminish. On the contrary, it kept increasing. The stories of tyrannical acts during the war were coming to light. The reports of the enquiry commissions were being published and old wounds were opened.

Many famous universities were making lucrative offers to Einstein. Most of his friends in Berlin suggested that he should stay in Berlin. Planck told him quite categorically that he must not leave Berlin.

In Britain, Eddington continued to experiment on the theories put forward by Einstein. Detailed discussions continued about the observations carried out during the solar eclipse. The Fellows of the Royal Society of Science and Royal Geological Societies gathered together on November 6, 1919. J.J. Thomson presided over it. Many physicists, mathematicians and geo-scientists were present. Many questions came up. It was discussed that they needed to do more elaborate research on the natural facts and theories which till then they had accepted with their eyes closed.

J.J. Thomson, who discovered the electron, said in his presidential speech that the latest Theory of Relativity given by Einstein was one of the greatest scientific achievements to date. The photographs during the solar eclipse were presented at this seminar and their experimental confirmation was done. The changes to Newton's theory, which had been prevalent for almost two hundred and fifty years, were also accepted.

On November 7, 1919, when Einstein woke up, his world was changed. He was in the headlines of all the newspapers. Long articles about his theories were written in The Times, Nature, etc.

That day, reporters had gathered at his place. Questions were raised about other facts along with scientific facts. Reporters asked him his views about the war. Another fact was also published that the practical verification of the scientific theories of Einstein, who was born in Germany, were done by the British scientists. As a result, there was no question of partiality. Another special thing was that the photographs that were taken that day were sold at high prices. A part of the income was spent on children who had become victims of the famine.

Even then there were many scientists who doubted Einstein's theories. In the minds of many people, Euclid and Newton had made such an impact that they were not ready to accept the new theory. Some people believed that the origin of the universe was just imagined according to the theories which were formulated earlier and wondered how the new theory explained the origin. A complex problem confronted scientists.

Einstein's life was full of anomalies. In the early stages, his work made British scientists forget that he was born in Germany. It was buried deep in the core of their hearts. When the time came to award Einstein the gold medal of the Royal Geological Society, the issue was highlighted. To start with, the majority were in Einstein's favour. Einstein started making preparations to go to England when he received a letter from Eddington. Lobbies against the Germans were very active. At the end, the proposal to honour Einstein was vetoed.

The intensity of the protest can be gauged from the fact that during that year no one was awarded a gold medal.

Letters of enquiries, invitations and challenges flowed in. Einstein's postman also got tired of delivering so many bundles of letters for him daily.

Several paper cuttings piled up. His reputation was gaining international acclaim. Mauzkowski prepared such a script about Einstein that it led to a controversy. Einstein's friends prohibited it from being published. In this book, distorted thoughts were expressed about science.

Einstein was always worried about lack of money. Now reputed newspapers were ready to give him thousands of dollars for just eight to ten page articles on his Theory of Relativity. People also wanted to see him as he was becoming an indispensable part of almost all newspapers. His photographs thus adorned the cover pages of the leading newspapers.

Another aspect was that people had been reading about the killings and destruction during the war for about five years. They hated news about bunkers, bombs and massacre. People wanted to forget the war and were looking for peace. Einstein's discovery and its approval by the scientists of the world became a subject of interest. Descriptions about this discovery, in which the bending of the rays of light was shown during the solar eclipse, etc. were the things that worked as a soothing ointment on the wounded minds of the people.

Praise was showered on Einstein outside Gemany too. The reaction within Germany was mixed. Scientists like Planck, Sommerfield, Haber, Nernst, etc. were influenced by his capabilities. Along with politicians, there were plenty of people who were jealous of him. They were not able to digest the international popularity of a Jew.

In his home city of Ulm, the people were proud of him. Generally people of his city believed that Albert had performed great wonders in physics. The local council passed a proposal and sent a resolution congratulating him. Einstein accepted the resolution. After two years, when Einstein's Nobel Prize was declared, the local city council of Ulm proposed to name a street after him, though the street chosen was on the outskirts of the city in a poor and backward area. The people of the city called him the 'Son of the City'. Much later, in 1949, they had sent a proposal asking him to become an honourable citizen of the city but Einstein refused.

Outside Germany, proceedings to honour him were in vogue. One after the other, many congratulatory letters were showered on him. A proposal was made to appoint him a special professor in which he would get a remuneration of 2,000 dollars annually. The appointment was for three years and he needed to visit the university only once or twice. It would not hamper his work in Berlin. By coincidence, this proposal was from the same place where twenty years ago Einstein's application for a job was rejected.

Einstein met Niels Bohr who had established the Institute of Theoretical Physics in Copenhagen. On Planck's request, he also delivered a lecture. There was a lot of difference between Einstein and Planck. Planck was well dressed and looked old, whereas Einstein's hair was black and he wore loose clothes.

Bohr was influenced by Einstein. A long scientific discussion took place between the two. At many places, Bohr proposed Einstein's name to give lectures.

In Germany, the constitution was changing. On July 1, 1920, Einstein had to take an oath to the new Constitution. After eight months, on March 15, 1921, he took the oath of the Prussian Constitution. He was always dissatisfied with the German citizenship imposed on him. Since his youth, he had expressed his hatred of German politics. He used to say that he wanted to be a member of the whole world.

In large parts of Germany, hatred was developing towards Einstein for his outspokenness. He was straightforward enough to say that those who won the world war had paid a great price for it. Anarchy was prevalent and people should use the progress made in science to rebuild Germany. The people of Germany had their own grudges owing to their defeat and feelings of patriotism. They were not prepared to believe those who talked about peace and universal brotherhood. A rally was organised in which the participants had put the symbol of the swastika upside down on their helmets. This swastika symbol is sacred in India.

The memories of atrocities carried out by the armies of the Alliance Nations were fresh in the minds of the Germans. They also had memories of scientists like Nernst and Haber who had participated in the war for their country. Einstein had been doing research related to theoretical physics even during the war. After gaining prestige, he was walking tall.

Obviously, talk against Einstein was gaining pace. Situations were changing fast. In his letters, Einstein openly protested against local activities. In Germany, the fight to acquire power was also increasing. In this situation, an agitation was started against Einstein.

Protests were made in different ways. Both his personality and his Theory of Relativity were attacked. Since he was a Jew, the number of people who hated him was plenty. Many strange reasons were given against him. Someone remarked that his Theory of Relativity was against the fundamental sentiments of the Germans. Many university teachers discussed the Theory of Relativity and started saying that it was useless. Seminars were often organised, in which the speaker not only said that the Theory of Relativity was wrong but also introduced it in a haphazard way. Moreover, it was remarked that it was unbalanced. They requested people not to accept it.

The most interesting thing was that Einstein himself participated in these seminars initially and enjoyed the annoyance of the speakers. He would laugh aloud and clap. After the seminars, he would thank the organisers for presenting an entertainment programme.

To answer the unscientific objections of his critics, Einstein took the support of the newspapers; this was seemingly an impossible thing at that time. Addressing people who objected to his Theory of Relativity he classified all these apprehensions. This step seemed so peculiar and dangerous at that time that even his close scientist friends were stunned. They felt that Einstein had been really very deeply hurt.

Reacting to the worries of his friends, Einstein said that it was essential for him to do so because even a young child in this city knew his face. So, it was imperative.

He found himself pressurised from both ends. On one side, those who were against him wanted him to leave Berlin. On the other side, his scientist friends in the university wanted him to stay in Germany. At the same time, he received an invitation from a British University.

Rumours of the controversy reached the ears of the education minister of Germany. In a letter to Einstein, he expressed his anxiety about the situation. Einstein gave a befitting reply but the controversy would not settle down. Whenever Einstein went to any seminar, he had to face a lot of interruptions.

Einstein now associated himself with people who were vociferous against a future war. He also participated in a procession in support of human rights in which about fifty to sixty thousand people had participated. Many people in Germany were planning the establishment of a republic. In this situation, Einstein decided that he would stay in Germany.

□

Post Nobel Prize

The campaign against the Jews started to gain momentum in Germany. Einstein got frequent invitations from abroad and he accepted them. But he did not like this excessive publicity. Wherever he went for lectures, huge audiences would gather there. In cities like Prague, Vienna, etc. there would be long queues of people asking him questions. Painters used to make his sketches during his lectures and request him to sign them. Once Einstein felt that a painter had made him look like a Chinese and he refused to sign it.

His wife, Elsa, took total care of him. She knew that the absent-minded husband of hers forgot everything.

Being in Germany in an anti-Jewish atmosphere, Einstein started something unique. He started establishing a Hebrew University in Jerusalem. Einstein took the responsibility to collect money for it. He decided to go to America to give special lectures there, so that whatever he earned could be utilised for the University. In February, 1921 he started getting invitations from America.

A problem now arose. Einstein had a limited knowledge of English and a bit of French. He proposed that he would speak only in German. He had gained so much popularity that even this proposal was accepted. He left for America in March 1921. At the same time, he received a similar proposal from England.

During this time, a change was seen in him. Einstein was alert during interviews. In America, he also addressed Jewish students and told them about the Hebrew University. He emphasised that the university was not just a matter of choice but was a matter of necessity.

Einstein went to England. He was full of zeal. He forgot that this was the country where the medal of the prestigious Royal Society was given to him and then snatched away. In England also he spoke in German. People listened to him with rapt attention and he was honoured with the title of Doctor of Sciences. This was a great happening in such a short time after the war.

In London, his host was Mr. Haldane. He had a great interest in Germany and also in Einstein. Haldane and he met with popular scientists like Eddington, J.J. Thomson and many others. In the post-war conditions, the journey of Einstein was like the journey of an ambassador. At many places while introducing Einstein, Haldane would say that Britain was grateful to Germany for giving a scientist like Einstein to the world, in the same way as Germany, on countless occasions, had shown its gratitude to Britain because Newton was born in England.

There were speculations that people would protest between the lectures due to his German origin. When the lectures proved to be successful, invitations also started coming from universities in Australia. Wherever Einstein went, the newspapers printed details about him, his scientific theories and his thoughts.

When he returned to Germany, he was regarded as the first German who had gone to the victorious Alliance Nations and created his place amongst them. Efforts were also being made to improve the situation in Germany. On July 1, 1921, Einstein participated in a feast organised by the German Red Cross Society. On this occasion, he spoke about the behaviour of scientists during his visits to America and Britain.

Even after receiving respect throughout the world, Einstein talked to people in a simple way. He used to forget that he was a world-famous personality. His talks were presented in different ways. He gained lots of respect. Many a times he used to say things in humour; spoken this way he was quite often misunderstood. At the feast of the Red Cross Society, he stated that England was pro-German and America anti-German. This comment was published by New York Times.

In the same way, he said that people of America were like pet dogs on which money was spent in incorrect and meaningless ways. This comment was also published in the New York Times. Rumours of such stories spread like wildfire and many people considered him anti-American. Einstein's friends tried to publish denials, but the correspondent once again remarked firmly that what was published before was the truth.

Slowly and gradually, the controversy intensified. An editorial of a newspaper mentioned that Dr. Einstein could never be pardoned because he had made a mockery of his American hosts. They had considered him a great personality and had extended him hospitality and honour. On the contrary, he had proved himself to be a man of low esteem. This could not be expected from such a popular scientist. By the time Einstein discovered that he had been misquoted, it was too late. Einstein did not get upset with this controversy. He continued his efforts to build a better relationship between German scientists and the Alliance Nations. In the beginning of 1922, he went to France. Earlier, he had been invited to visit France in 1913. Due to the World War, he was not able to go there.

Many people observed that he might face opposition in France since he was a German. A French minister, who was also a renowned mathematician, was in favour of inviting him. Many powerful people respected and supported Einstein whole-heartedly. So, he did not have any difficulty in going to France.

After his visit to France, Einstein went to Belgium. Now he became the centre of attraction not only for scientists but also for literary people who described his looks and features interestingly.

Once astronomer Charles Nordmann accompanied Einstein. The literary talent in him sprouted and he described in a beautiful way Einstein's looks, features and even his shoulders. He described his eyes, nose, and chin, etc. as though he had been describing a film star for a magazine article.

People even listened to his philosophical thoughts. Einstein had linked his Theory of Relativity with philosophy and presented it in a philosophical way. However, along with the reception, ceremonies and celebrations, protests against him continued. The League of Nations had been formed. Peace efforts had been made under its banner. But Germany did not become its member. During his journey to France, Einstein had to face protests on this count. One day, when Einstein entered the lecture room, three members of the French Academy walked out. The French media also differed in opinion during Einstein's visit. France had to bear more loss as compared to Britain. Memories were still fresh. In the war, about 13,50,000 people had died or were missing. Einstein also had an idea regarding it. On his last day in France, he visited the war-fields. He saw the areas affected by German attacks. He saw the villages that had been destroyed and wore a deserted look. Bunkers had been made at many places. Entire forests had been blown up.

Einstein shivered at the sights. Seeing the evidences of devastation done by the war, Einstein felt how much worse it must have been while the war was on.

At one place, when he saw the farms and trees destroyed by poison gas, he writhed in pain and said, "Every student of Germany should be brought here to see it. Why Germans only? Students from all over the world should be brought here and shown these ghastly acts. People have a different conception of war. Literature and books are not enough to describe war. Only after seeing the destruction, one can visualise the reality though not the complete reality."

Einstein visited many war-fields and saw the scenes of destruction. After that, he found words insufficient to express his feelings. He stopped at a place for lunch. When he finished his lunch, two French military officers, who had been sitting on a bench and were in uniform, rose and saluted Einstein. They had been noticing him for quite a long time and recognised him.

During this period, a film had been made based on Einstein's Theory of Relativity. Before this film could become a success, it created a controversy. Einstein remarked that he had no hand in the creation of the film and also he did not agree with its title. However, the film was successful and its screening crossed the Atlantic Ocean and was shown in distant countries.

After his visit to France, Einstein received many invitations. By the time he received an invitation from

Zurich, the situation in Germany had deteriorated. Walther Rathenau, a liberal leader and a prominent well-wisher of Einstein, was killed on June 24, 1922 by the extremists of the Right Wing. He was a Jew by origin. Before him, another Jewish leader was attacked and severely injured.

Walther Rathenau had become the foreign minister just a few months ago. Despite being his friend, Einstein wasn't happy about his becoming a minister. Perhaps, he had a premonition about Rathenau's future. Just after becoming minister, Rathenau was able to open diplomatic relations with Russia. Economic co-operation between the two had started. This happened without the knowledge of America, Britain and France. Many people felt that the present German Government was moving towards Jewish communism. Dividing lines became prominent.

The murder of Rathenau made this division more apparent. When the last rites of Rathenau were performed, national mourning was declared and all schools, colleges and universities were ordered to remain closed. But some people deliberately continued their activities. During this period, people realised Einstein was also a Jew and, being a close associate of Rathenau, they feared that he might be the next target of the murderers.

These rumours were not baseless. A year ago when Einstein had gone to America and gained unbelievable popularity there, in Berlin a German youth had taken a pledge to kill Einstein. Many scholars and university professors were very irritated by the Jews, including Einstein, and openly commented that if these people were shot dead it would be a service to the country. Later, the youth was arrested but was given a light punishment.

Einstein was quite aware of these developments. He had pointed to these in the letter written to Madame Curie on

July 4. Now, he rejected invitations for lectures. Explaining, he wrote to Max Planck that now his stay in Berlin would not be safe. His presence in public places anywhere could lead to untoward incidents.

But there were people who inspired him to live a normal public life and continue his activities. Madame Curie wrote a letter to him and requested him to remain in the League Commission. She said that by doing so he would honour the memory of Rathenau.

Einstein became more enthusiastic. Once he said that it had become almost impossible to work as an intellectual in the German community or the international community. He liked these exciting moments and he was ready to face any situation.

People still tried to persuade him to give lectures. As the rumour spread that Einstein was coming for a lecture, the group, which was against his Theory of Relativity, became active. They distributed pamphlets and made critical remarks against him.

In 1922, he was selected for the Nobel Prize. Though this award should have been given to him many years ago, still it acted like a catalyst for protests against him in Germany. The most notable thing was that though his Theory of Relativity was quite famous, yet he was given the Nobel Prize for the photo electric effect. Einstein had explained the emission of electrons in the beginning of 1920.

The announcement of the Nobel Prize invited bitter criticism. One scientist wrote a letter to the Swedish Academy accusing it of giving more importance to Einstein, "whereas his Theory of Relativity was full of loopholes."

On the other side in Stockholm, both the German and Swiss embassies claimed Einstein as their citizen. Another controversy was: which ambassador would have the honour of standing beside him at the Award ceremony. A series of accusations and counter-accusations started. This was important because at the Nobel Prize distribution ceremony, the King of Sweden himself presented the royal bouquet.

Both the countries started pressing Einstein. Conflicts deepened. Finally on the day of the Award ceremony, December 11, the death anniversary of Alfred Nobel, Einstein remained outside Europe and was not able to receive the Award in person. In his place, the German Ambassador received the award and gave it to the Swiss Ambassador who handed the prize over to Einstein in Berlin. Einstein had given his approval for this arrangement.

In this situation, anomalies and controversies arose once again regarding his citizenship. On January 13, 1923, the German Science Minister gave an order that every person in government service would be deemed to be a German citizen. That rule made Einstein a German, retrospective from 1914.

On the other hand, Einstein repeatedly denied his being a German citizen. On May 14, 1923 a German minister wrote to him a firm letter and suggested that he should meet a senior officer if he had any doubt about his citizenship. Responding to the letter, after six months Einstein met the officer. At the meeting, it was again clarified that he was a German citizen.

Although Einstein was not able to receive the Award in person and the money went directly to Mileva, yet his economic condition improved. Not only did people stand in queue for his lectures but publishers approached him for his compositions with proposals of good remuneration.

A number of people wanted to deceive the simple Einstein. One Japanese publisher acquired his expensive research works at a paltry amount. Invitations poured in for Einstein from distant China and Japan. Good translators were found for his lectures, who could explain his works to the local people. Einstein was very impressed by Japan. The people and their behaviour appeared very pleasant. Japan was a beautiful country with well-mannered people.

While returning from Japan, Einstein halted at Palestine where the construction of the Hebrew University had started five years ago. He was very attached to it. He then went to Spain with Elsa.

King Alfonso XIII heard his lectures at the Science Academy there. The Rector of Madrid University made a proposal that not only Einstein but also his son should be given the title of honorary doctorate. The Education Minister of Spain made a proposal for a house for Einstein. During this time, he heard that on March 20, the Citizen Council of Ulm had named one more street after him.

It was not in Einstein's destiny to avoid controversies. Before coming to Madrid, he had addressed an assembly of workers in Barcelona. These workers were in favour of direct action to get hold of industries. Some portions of Einstein's lectures were published in The Times, which remarked that not only was he a revolutionary but he was striving to bring about revolution in the field of science.

There was nothing wrong with this statement. Yet the pro-leftist newspapers published it with extra punch. At last, Einstein had to clarify his position.

When Einstein reached Berlin, he got the news that his theory had been proved true in the last solar eclipse and now there was no need to be confused. Both pro-Einstein and anti-Einstein groups of scientists had taken interest in it. The results of this experiment were published all over the world - from America to Australia. Weather during the solar eclipse was also good and better photographs had been taken. On September 21, 1922, The Times published a detailed report on it, and the bending of the rays of light was shown.

After returning to Germany, Einstein felt that he had done enough travelling. So, he decided to stay at one place. Conditions also seemed better. But he received an invitation from Russia.

On September 15, 1923, it was announced in a newspaper that Einstein was going to Russia. Along with it, stories were being circulated about his journey.

The rumours about the strained relationship between the German government and the leftists had already spread. Germans felt that Russia was trying to take the Jews under their influence. The situation of hatred increased so much that when Einstein went to the house of a Jewish friend for dinner, he was advised not to go home that night, because there was a great danger to his life. His other friends like Planck, etc. were also anxious about him.

In between, Einstein went to Holland and returned in November 1923. People used to visit him frequently after he had got the Nobel Prize. Among them were some very affluent people. But Einstein was not affected by this popularity. Proposals to honour him came from Japan in the East and America in the West.

But Einstein had a different dream in his mind. He wanted to free the Motherland of the Jews. This place was called Palestine. He wanted to build a new Europe, in which peace would prevail everywhere. He wanted to see the whole world bound together in a single thread.

He had political aspirations in his mind. His scientist friends like Rutherford and Madame Curie wanted him to limit himself to the scientific field.

His name was used in several small and large endeavours. Wealthy Jews used to donate big amounts in his name for the future Israel. People who desired peace used his name for their effort.

Though Einstein knew that the extremists were against these campaigns and they had been opposing Einstein in different ways, yet he remained indifferent to these aspects.

□

Changing Circumstances

Conditions in Germany were changing rapidly. After the war, the economic conditions had deteriorated rapidly. Now the conditions were more stable. The whole world was facing a period of recession and was getting into the grip of famine.

Changing circumstances can be seen from the fact that before the war, the salary of a physics professor in Kaiser Wilhelm Institute was 75,000 marks which was equivalent to 17,750 dollars. After the war, it was reduced to 22,000 marks which was equivalent to 1,125 dollars. Every professor was compelled to work at twenty per cent of his original salary.

Owing to lack of money, very few scientific meetings could be organised. It had become difficult for the professors to make regular payments to their assistants. When lectures were organised, people were not able to attend them due to high transport costs.

But Einstein's condition was quite different. His books were selling incessantly and a substantial amount of royalty was coming to him. His wealthy industrialist friends willingly deposited money in his account. Now he had no problem to pay his assistants their salaries. Einstein lived in his house in Berlin. The house was nice, comparatively bigger and well arranged. Elsa had made his life smooth. Not only this, his step-daughter - Elsa's daughter - worked as his secretary.

Einstein spent most of his time in his reading room, where he had only books in front of him. There was a round table in the room and there were paper, pencils, notes, slips, etc. in the cupboard.

Einstein had the habit of smoking cigar. His wife always tried to keep him under control. As a result, Einstein used to hide the cigar box in the cover of a book. The friends who visited him used to bring cigars for him. In this way, he filled the cigar box again. The reading room remained dirty because he did not permit anyone to tidy it. He did not even like his wife to enter it. He could tolerate the dust and dirt but he never tolerated interference. Another strange thing was that he called his wife 'my old lady'.

Einstein spent his mornings in the room. Often in the evening, when he didn't have lecture assignments, he liked to sit there. He could think, write and calculate. Thoughts of the rotation of the planets, the speed of the light emitted by stars shining like diamonds, the lightness of hydrogen, the usability of radium, would rotate in his mind. Sometimes, he thought about the flow of electricity in wires and sometimes about the heaviness of lead. Infinite thought about matter, energy, time, infinity occupied his mind.

The number of books based on his theory of relativity was increasing. Every year, extensive research papers and articles were being prepared on this subject. In Germany alone, 14 editions of one of his books were printed and

65,000 copies sold. Just in 19 months, seven English versions were printed. Slowly, people got the correct picture of his Theory of Relativity. In 1925, a well-known writer, Bertrand Russell wrote a book giving elementary and fundamental knowledge about relativity. His intention was to provide the common people with the appropriate information. Einstein and Russell had many things in common. They had many differences also. Still, they remained good friends.

Many people paid attention to Einstein's ideology. Einstein helped those with similar thoughts in all possible ways. He gave his time to them and also spent money on them. Once a young student of chemical science from abroad came to Bonn for studies, but he did not get admission. According to the rules, nobody could apply for a second time. That boy asked Einstein for help. Einstein through his influence got him admitted. It was considered an impossible task at that time.

In the same way, he also helped a student from Poland. He was also a Jew. At that time, circumstances were in favour of refugees from Poland, especially the Jews. Hesitatingly, the student pressed the doorbell of Einstein's house. He was wondering how this renowned physicist would behave with him. Einstein met him with joy and gave him a recommendation letter which proved useful to him.

But Einstein was not, at all, interested in social ceremonies. He hated to be the chief guest. He was quite conscious of wearing clothes in accordance with the function. He liked to live in freedom.

Industrialists were very impressed by Einstein. It seemed to them that this physicist could provide them with unusual help. Einstein also utilised his connections with the industrialists. One industrialist, Dr. Bosch gave grants to an institute on Einstein's insistence. This institute carried forward the programme of experimental testing of Einstein's theory related to relativity. Later, an observatory was also made there for research related to the composition of the solar system. A huge telescope was fixed on a sixty foot tower. Another special tower was near it, where the rays of the sun used to turn at an angle of 90 degrees. Its design was magnificent and people started calling it the 'Einstein Tower'. Its composition was such that it seemed as though the designer had known about the composition of atoms and mathematical equations. The composition was quite evident in the tower. Even today, people come to see it.

Everybody did not like this structure. To several people, this building seemed like a combination of the pyramids of Egypt and the tall buildings of New York. It was also said to be against German tradition. During that anti-Jew period, several criticisms were made.

Einstein had almost stopped teaching. His office had become more spacious. Every thursday afternoon he used to organise seminars, in which he not only spoke but also listened to brilliant students of Physics. He sat in the first row in the seminars and a cigar was always in his hand. He used to attend other seminars and participated in the discussions related to Physics. He often used a blackboard to explain what he had said.

At the same time, he conducted many activities. He fulfilled all those responsibilities related to the universities, which he had willingly accepted. He worked at Potsdam Observatory and also at the Kaiser Wilhelm Institute. He participated in scientific seminars. Reputed scientists like Niels Bohr, etc. were his guests.

He went on tours for the sake of social work. He always carried the violin with him. He frequently visited Max Planck's house for dinner and listened to the piano played by him after dinner. Every type of person, artist, industrialist, literary, etc. was among his friends. He often said, "Nature has given us lots of comfort to enjoy and we should not ignore them."

He was not bound to time. Whenever he felt hungry, he ate. Whenever he got tired, he slept. There was a table in his dining room which was always full of milk, bread, cheese, fruits etc. He abstained from material comforts. Manuscripts, violin, bed, table, chair, etc. were more than enough for him.

Einstein avoided accepting formal gifts from rich people. Once Queen Wilhelmina came with the Prince and the royal family and expressed her desire to meet Einstein. With great difficulty, Einstein was able to fulfill this formality. He wanted to sneak out quietly from there, but in vain. The Queen noticed this act of his. She revealed it in front of everyone.

With the passage of time, Einstein started to pay more attention to the Jews. His special interest was the establishment of the Hebrew University. In 1925, he faced an obstacle. He had to go to South America to deliver his lectures. For this, he even sacrificed an invitation from the California Institute of Technology in America. His friends believed that had he accepted that invitation because he wanted to spend the last two decades of his life there.

In a real sense, the decade of the 1920s was very important for Physics. Many theories were developed, nurtured and proved during the period. Planck's quantum theory, Einstein's theory related to the photon, Rutherford's nuclear theory and Bohr's atomic theory, all these had started to spread their wings over the whole scientific world. Old beliefs were rapidly being destroyed. Not only ordinary students, but specialists also felt that, till then, they had thought they knew everything, but what they knew was not correct. They wondered whether what was being discovered currently would hold true in future or not.

Great scientists are a determined lot. J.J. Thomson proved the existence of electrons in such a way as if it had been visible to the naked eye. The world, from the atomic age, had entered the nuclear age. It had become easy for researchers to avail themselves of a doctorate. Now, there was an abundance of subjects. But the ordinary students felt deceived.

□

In touch with an Indian Research Student

Far away in India, in the University of Dhaka, a young scientist named Satyendranath Bose was doing unusual research in Physics. In 1924, he sent Einstein a research paper related to Planck's theory and the quantum theory of light. In the paper, he described radiation as a gas consisting of photons.

Einstein read this research paper and was so impressed that he himself translated it into German and sent it to the editor of a German magazine. In July 1924, this research paper was published. He was quite impressed by Bose's methods relating to a number of equations. He believed that with these methods it would be easier to study the characteristics of atoms. Later, this method was to be called the 'Bose-Einstein Equation'.

In the same way research scholars like De Broglie, Shrodeinger, etc. developed new theories and equations. The theories they developed still hold ground.

Several jokes were also being made regarding the upcoming nuclear age. New theories were creating complications. Scientists were criticising one another's theories. Some were very happy with the ongoing developments, but most of them were upset.

During this period, Einstein took the support of humour quite often. He compared the changes in the theories in physics to the changes in fashion. He used to present his new formula E = mc2 in an interesting way. He never missed the opportunity to comment on the existence of God. According to him, God did not create this world by throwing a dice, meaning that God did not create this world in a whimsical fashion. Anyway, if it is to be believed that God created this world, He must have done it according to the rules of Nature.

At that time, whenever there were discussions on the theory of science, the atmosphere would become tense. At such moments, Einstein cracked jokes to relieve the tension. If a controversy arose regarding a research paper of a scientist, he would crack a joke and lighten the atmosphere. Young and emerging scientists were quite impressed by him.

After Einstein's discovery, Newton's discovery paled. But Einstein had a remarkable respect for Newton. When a function was organised in Newton's honour in England, Einstein sent in his best wishes.

Einstein was now giving less time to Physics and was spending most of his time working for the Jews—establishment of peace and the Hebrew University. Along with that, he was trying to explain the composition of the atom to those people, who were not specialists.

One more incident occurred during this period. Einstein was returning after delivering a lecture. He had a big, heavy suitcase with him, but he did not hire a porter. Snow was falling and the road had become slippery. Suddenly, Einstein slipped. He was taken to a hospital, where he was treated without much success.

Later he was taken to Dr. Flash. By origin, Dr Flash was a Hungarian. He was a well-known doctor in Berlin. Along with medical science, he had an interest in theatre and diplomacy. He examined Einstein thoroughly and said that the walls of his heart showed some infection. He prohibited intake of salt and instructed his wife to take him to some resort near the sea and give him complete rest.

But Einstein did not pay attention to the doctor's advice. Sometimes he used to go for boating. Later Dr. Flash totally prohibited it. Slowly, he regained his health.

But Einstein did not give up his way of working. He decided to keep a secretary so that some of his work might be shared. The question arose whether he should give an advertisement in the newspaper. But there was the risk that lots of candidates would apply and it would hamper his rest. At last, Elsa found a way and contacted the acting secretary of a Jewish orphanage. Elsa was the President of this orphanage. Finally, the secretary's sister, Helen Dukas came to meet him for this purpose.

Helen Dukas was reluctant. She had no knowledge of Physics. However, Einstein wanted to engage her because it was not possible for him to work without a secretary any more. After much persuasion, Helen agreed.

Along with his correspondence, she handled his other works also. Helen's relationship with Einstein deepened.

Circumstances were changing rapidly. It was impossible for Einstein to participate in every seminar due to ill-health. It was dangerous with regard to security also. Helen had to find options several times so that the organisers might not get disheartened. Germany was moving towards a war. The country had come under severe unemployment. The industrialists were apprehensive about the spread of communism. Anti-Jewish feelings were at their height. Hitler's political party was gaining strength in the country. □

Efforts for Peace

Einstein was nearing fifty. How much the peace-lovers liked him was evident from the fact that they used to record his messages and deliver them to large audiences at their meetings. During this period, his books on peace were published.

The number of people who wanted peace was increasing. People in several countries were still terror stricken by the bloodshed of World War I. They were making efforts for peace in their own ways. In such a situation, Einstein's comments, interviews and articles received wide publicity.

By this time the League of Nations, which was formed to establish peace after World War I, had become ineffective. This increased the courage of the warmongers, especially Hitler.

But the supporters of peace were also numerous. They were in a good number, not only in Germany, but spread all across Europe. Along with Einstein, everyone had a lot of hope in the League. Then, in 1922, to get Einstein's support, Sir Eric Drummond, the Chief Secretary of the

League, invited him to become a member of the International Committee, which was formed under the League.

Controversy started on the question of giving membership to Einstein. People questioned whether Einstein was the true representative of German culture. Germany had still not become a member of the League. Later, he was accorded membership on the basis that he represented German science world. At that time several French officers strongly opposed him and maintained that a person of German origin should not be made its member. Many questions were raised on his being a German. They also complained that he was a Swiss Jew. The victorious Alliance Nations had an upper hand in the League. They were not in favour of allowing anyone who was vociferous and impartial to play an important role.

After hearing everything, Einstein accepted the invitation to become its member in 1922. He informed Madame Curie. She had also been made a member. Many intellectuals such as Lorentz, Gilbert Marey, etc. were also made member.

In Berlin, the Jews were being advised to abstain from active politics. When he became a member, member to represent Germany, local protests started. In July 1922, Einstein decided to renounce this membership. So, he sent a resignation letter.

Along with Madame Curie, many others felt very upset about it. Einstein had not mentioned any reason in his resignation letter. Efforts to make him retract proved to be an exercise in futility. At last, the resignation letter was accepted. Most of the professors in Germany refused to take his place on the committee because Germany was still not in the League.

Conditions in Germany were deteriorating. Inflation was increasing rapidly. At the end of 1922, the Weimar

Government in Germany refused to pay the amount imposed on it as penalty for World War I. So, France tried to capture a part of the industrial area of Germany. They felt that undue importance was being given to Albert Einstein.

At last, on July 25, 1924, Einstein was introduced as a new member of the Committee.

During that time, Einstein continued giving suggestions which differed from prevailing trends. He believed that the scientists and the artists were keeping themselves bound into narrow nationalism, whereas their main responsibility should be towards the public. In the meantime, an International Organisation was formed for moral support. France collected finances for it. This made it certain that only a French person would head this organisation located in Paris. Einstein had his own doubts. He himself wanted to protest but he had to go to South America. He pressurised Lorentz to protest, but Lorentz did not heed his words.

Einstein continued to participate in the meetings of the International Committee. He suggested that if scientific instruments and books of any scientist would get destroyed due to war, he should be helped so that he might restart his work. The committee did not have any financial support, but there was general satisfaction; scientists like Einstein, Lorentz and Madame Curie were thinking about such matters.

Einstein was also a member of many sub-committees which were preparing the data for several subjects and were working on the formation of a proposed Weather Bureau. He suggested allotment of the money given by the Red Cross to learned persons in Russia and also emphasised efforts to establish peace in future with the help of school education.

Overall, he was not satisfied with the work of the Committee. His main concern was to remove the causes that led to misunderstanding and hatred. They not only increased the probability of war but also made it popular.

According to him, "If the League could increase the quality of education in the world, no other service was better than this." He used to put forward his suggestions with great clarity and passion.

Among his remarkable suggestions, education was for the growth and he emphasised in this during his regular discussions with the philosophers of the world. Matters related to a particular subject, like history, should also be included and a collection of these thoughts should be published. The first part 'A League of Mind' was even published. Einstein's views were also demanded for the second part.

Einstein willingly provided his suggestions. One suggestion was to review the history books of France and Germany in such a way that false information and facts which increased the feeling of enmity between the people of both countries could be removed. He put a lot of stress on the psychological analysis of the minds of children to inculcate a desire for world peace in them. He also suggested suppression of those patterns of thinking that gave rise to thoughts that later became conflicts.

Einstein had an extended correspondence with Freud. Later, this correspondence was published in German and French under the titles Law and Violence and Why Wars respectively. But their publication was banned in Germany. Even permission for advertising for these works was denied.

The situation in the world was deteriorating. One reason was that the Pacifists themselves were confused. Einstein's two statements often contradicted each other. In 1920, Einstein unconditionally supported peace. Later, he introduced conditions for peace. He believed that dictators like Hitler and Mussolini could only be controlled by the use of weapons. Initially, his message was that everybody should abstain from any type of war-like activities and should not support any type of war activities overtly or covertly.

In 1926, Germany became a member of the League and a National Committee was formed in Germany to co-ordinate with the League. Einstein was made a member. Einstein put up questions about cultural atrocities on minorities. He felt that efforts towards education were still immature and those people who were working unconditionally to build world peace were not getting support.

In February, 1932, a disarmament conference started. Sixty countries participated in it. The countries which were not formal members of the League were allowed to participate. Russia and the U.S.A. also participated. Though there was not much expectation from the conference, yet Einstein still appreciated it.

After this conference, leg pulling of one another continued for months. Emphasis was given on using weapons against weapons to maintain balance. Einstein was upset about this. He clearly believed that every country should honestly and totally destroy all its weapons. It should hand over its future to an international organisation.

On January 23, 1932, Einstein entered the office of the League early in the morning to see Japanese and Russian representatives debating about increasing the presence and activities of aircraft carriers. American and British representatives were having a similar sort of discussion. Everyone became silent on seeing Einstein. Perhaps, his personality emitted such radiation that it dazzled everyone. They forgot their work and stared at him.

On May 22, 1932, Einstein set out for Geneva from London. A famous pacifist, Lord Ponsonby, was also with him. He was a close friend of Arthur Henderson, who presided over this conference.

That same afternoon, Einstein organised a conference in the Bergius Hotel, in which about sixty reporters participated. His messages for peace were published and were given lot of publicity. Einstein clearly said, "In whatever way the rules of war are made, humanity will be destroyed in it. So, it is very necessary to destroy the war itself. People should stop serving in the army."

Many people thought this suggestion was unusual. But Einstein remained firm in what he had said. He stated clearly that the war was comedy for some people, but it was a matter of sorrow for most. We should stop it in any way we could. We should apply every possible way to do so. To stop the war, everything concerned with it, i.e. production of weapons and its export and import, should be stopped. People would have to abandon jobs in the army. If the workers of the world abstained from work related to the preparation of the war, the possibility of the war would automatically become extinct.

That could not be done by the governments; it was only the people who could do it. Governments did not know what people wanted and what problems they faced. The people in the government were just puppets in the hands of the weapons manufacturers. When Einstein advanced his view, he seemed very excited. The statesmen sang different tunes. Before disarmament, France was talking about general security. The opinion to boycott such seminars was developing strongly in Germany.

□

Love for the Jews

The modern Jewish movement started in 1897 and it slowly spread all over the world wherever the Jews lived. Their powers and positions were different in different places. At some places, power was indirectly in their hands, but at other places, they were very weak and were tortured in different ways.

At the Congress of the Jews, which took place at Bessel in 1897, it was decided that like other communities there should be a motherland for the Jews. So the area of present Palestine was selected. The father of this movement was Theodore Hurl. Hurl died in 1904. Now Germany became the centre of this movement. In the beginning, it was active in Cologne and, later, it became active in Berlin. There were several controversies over the site of the motherland. The British government made a proposal to give an area of 6,000 miles in East Africa to the Jews, but the Jews rejected it. Most of the Jews were in favour of Palestine.

Palestine had been in the possession of the Turks for centuries. In 1908, a revolution took place in Turkey against giving lands to the Jews and it started appearing that Turkey would not abandon that place for the Jews. It also looked as though the movement started by Hurl had come to a halt.

The Jews themselves were not united. Some were quite powerful and rich in their respective areas. Some were quite orthodox as regards their beliefs and traditions. Some used to say clearly that the Jews were an affluent community and should have their own country. Some were busy with their business.

Since his childhood, Einstein had no feelings about being a Jew. In 1914, he accepted openly that he was a Jew. In fact, most of the Jews in Germany tried to hide their identities.

In 1917, the British Foreign Minister said that his Government was in favour of creating a country for the Jews in Palestine. It was also prepared to take some action to achieve it.

This was during World War I. The Alliance Nations were in desperate need of money. The entire system of giving loans was in the hands of the Jews. Ancient Palestine was rising in a new way after 1,300 years of rule by Persia and Turkey. This suddenly increased the aspirations of the Jews.

After World War I, these hopes began to decline. After the war, the enmity between the Germans and the Jews became intense. Einstein's views and those of other Jews like him, rapidly spread not only in Germany, but throughout the Europe.

After coming to Switzerland from Berlin, Einstein became aware of the problems faced by young Jews. When the governments changed after the war, these problems increased further. Some Jews became homeless. Einstein made special arrangements for the study of these distressed Jewish students, which got recognition from the government.

During that time Einstein developed the idea of establishing a Hebrew University. He felt that the university which would be run by the Jews for the Jews could perform a magnificent task. Einstein's Judaism took shape.

In 1919, Einstein began to participate actively in the Jewish movement. The Jews started to get support from this famous scientist. During this period, Kurt Blumenfeld played a key role in the Jewish movement. He met Einstein in February 1919. Einstein raised several questions at this meeting. He asked about the benefit to the Jews from the Jewish Movement, whether they would get internal security or not.

He had many anxieties in mind—the Jews had been living without a country for centuries. They were efficient enough to do scientific and other difficult work on their own. What was the necessity of a separate country?

Blumenfeld did not get upset by his apprehensions and questions. They met a second time. In the meantime, a friend of Einstein tried to draw his attention towards the Bible, but Einstein did not show any interest in it. Slowly, Einstein kept himself aloof from the nationalism that was developing in Germany. He inclined more towards the Jewish Movement.

The complex circumstances which were changing also encouraged him to move closer to the Jews. Many people in Germany believed that the Jews were responsible for the Russian revolution. They believed the Jews to be more dangerous. Many friends of Einstein advised him not to get involved in this movement and to give more attention to his scientific work, as the movement would cause severe damage to the Jews of Germany. When a talk about creating a country for the Jews outside Europe was initiated, everyone asked, "Why not send all the Jews there?"

The controversy became so intense that even Einstein got upset. Later, his thoughts became firm. He stated, "If people say that those Jews who live in Germany and work for the Jews and the creation of a Jewish nation in Palestine, can't be Germans, how can then the Jews be the Jews if they don't work for their own people and their own country? A man should always be honest about his origin, community and traditions. If he can't be loyal to these things, how can he be loyal to the country in which he is living?"

The patrons of the Jews were steadily implanting Jewish ideas in Einstein's mind. They wanted to fill his blood with love for the Jews before using him for publicity for their movement. They did not want to plant words in his mouth; they wanted the words to come automatically from his mouth.

Many Jews were dispersed due to war; they had settled in different countries. In a short time, they gained acceptance due to their talents. Chaim Weizmann was one such Jew of Russian origin. Just before World War I, he had settled in England and made a name for himself in the scientific world. Biochemist Weizmann developed the chemical bomb for the war. When the war started, he got a government job in Manchester University. Later, he was made the Director of the Naval Laboratory.

Weizmann's influence was increasing in the British Government. Due to his suggestion, the Government agreed to the idea of a separate nation for the Jews in Palestine. To the powerful Weizmann, Einstein looked like a very impractical person. Despite this, they were good friends.

The Jews also had a controversy regarding the nature of the new Jewish country. Many orthodox Jews wanted the new country to be politically strong. They were struggling against the Arabs situated nearby. Einstein favoured the principle of 'live and let live'. He wanted to make the new country a strong cultural centre. His main motive was that Jewish students from the entire world should gather there and receive education. He wanted to prevent any possible opposition from the Arabs.

While Weizmann was collecting funds for the establishment of a Jewish nation, Einstein was collecting funds for the establishment of the Hebrew University. The Jews were so enthusiastic and their fund collection drive received momentum. One politician fixed the target at 5 lakh dollars annually, whereas Weizmann increased it to one crore dollars annually. But it did not improve Weizmann's image. Many European Jews considered Weizmann a dictator.

Both Einstein and Weizmann set out for America on the same ship. During this journey in 1921, Mrs. Weizmann was quite impressed by Einstein. There were also some discussions between Weizmann and Einstein about the elements of Physics. Apart from this, they discussed seriously the probable ways of developing a Jewish movement in America.

As soon as the ship reached the American harbour, reporters and cameramen surrounded him. This was a new experience for Einstein because he had never experienced such popularity in Germany. But Einstein did not get nervous. He was questioned about the Theory of Relativity and he was asked to explain it in a few words. Einstein replied promptly, "Why not? But you should not take this answer seriously and consider it just as a joke." Einstein continued, "Previously it was believed that when everything in this world was destroyed, time and space would continue to exist. According to the theory of relativity, they will also be destroyed."

After visiting America, Einstein became more confident. He always kept smiling. His hair, collar and tie used to shine.

Many people were eager to know whether Elsa Einstein had understood the theory of relativity or not. Elsa would reply, "No, though Albert has tried several times to make me understand."

They were also eager to know about his daily activities. Elsa explained about Einstein's passion for playing the violin. She said that Albert worked day and night to formulate any theory.

Having arrived in New York, he saw that the Jews had decorated their place very beautifully. Jewish slogans and Jewish flags were on show. At that time, the Jewish flag had only two colours (white and blue). The Star of David which is used today was not a part of the flag.

At the venue of the seminar, Einstein had worn a brown overcoat and black trousers. In one hand, he had a pipe and in the other, a violin. He seemed more like a musician than a scientist. He was of medium height and had a strong body, wide forehead and shining eyes. His face reflected innocence, simplicity and dispassion.

Einstein and Weizmann, along with their wives, were taken to the city Hall under full security. At the City Hall, about five thousand Jews waited to greet them. But Einstein's mind was occupied with his own thoughts. He wanted to collect as much funds as he could for the Hebrew University. He wanted to impress the intellectuals of America by giving them information about his Theory of Relativity so that a positive environment might be formed to fulfill his aim.

There was good co-ordination between Einstein and Weizmann during this trip. Both addressed a crowd of eight thousand Jews on April 12. But some statements by Weizmann created a controversy and Einstein started to keep distance from him. However, due to their efforts, the funds continued to increase. At a meeting on April 20, they collected 26,000 dollars besides assurances for one lakh dollars. The dedication of the Jews was evident from the queue (of donors) that was formed to give funds. One old person brought 1000 dollars in a sack. The dollars were in the form of coins. This was his life's saving.

Einstein never forgot to mention the Hebrew University in his speeches. He used to say that it would be the greatest thing after the decline of Jerusalem and would prove very useful to the Jews. He also mentioned the problems of the Jews of Germany. His words had such an effect on the people that the American Jews became his disciples and the first donation he received was a huge amount of 10,000 dollars.

Between all these activities, the lectures given by Einstein on relativity were marvellous. Sometimes, he talked with the audience in an unusual way and he interacted with equal regard with everyone, whether the President or a common man. He also used to draw figures on blackboards to clarify his words. His frequent jokes endeared him to his listeners all the more.

On his return journey, Einstein was alone because Weizmann stayed back in America for his mission. When he returned from his last lecture, the Jews of Queensland had closed their shops in his honour and a convoy of 200 cars along with a band in the front row accompanied him. The crowd was so curious that the safety of Einstein and Weizmann was endangered.

With this trip, the dream of a Jewish nation started to flourish. Einstein was more impressed by the American Jews than they were impressed by him. The Jews who were settled in America had mostly migrated from Russia, Poland and Eastern Europe. They had an unquestionable devotion and dedication to their community.

The most significant outcome of this journey was that now the Hebrew University fund had enough money.

Another fact was that the middle class Jews had given more donations than the upper class ones. Some problems also arose. About 20,000 dollars had been pledged in a club in Boston, but only 4,000 dollars were received. On Weizmann's request, Einstein wrote a letter to the club. One more discrepancy was detected. Weizmann felt the trip was a failure since he had fixed a greater target. Einstein, on the other hand, was satisfied.

Journey to Palestine

After his successful trip to America, he planned that on his way back from his trip to the Eastern World he would visit Palestine. Palestine had been in the possession of Turkey and was now in the hands of the British. The League of Nations had given its approval for the establishment of an independent nation for the Jews. The British High Commission was already established there. On Einstein's visit, arrangements were made for his stay with the British High Commissioner, Sir Herbert. Sir Herbert was a philosopher and a politician. Interestingly, he was a Jew and the British government had appointed him out of respect for the Jews. He was aware of the effect of Einstein's Theory of Relativity and was apprehensive about the probable Jewish-Arab conflict.

On February 2, 1923, Einstein reached Tel Aviv with Elsa. There he was greeted by Colonel Frederick Kisch, who had retired from the army after his magnificent performance in the war. He, too, was active in the Jewish movement.

Einstein, who was considered to be the best and most controversial scientist, gave rise to a fresh controversy on his visit. He stated that learning Hebrew was unproductive for his mind.

Despite this, a grand reception was organised for him. Both sides of the path were crowded by people and especially children, who welcomed him. Many times, the enthusiastic crowds became restless and chaotic.

Einstein gave his historic speech at the Hebrew University. He was informed about the political situation of the place and he was told that this was the site where five years ago, British and Turkish cannons opened fire on each other. In future, there was a probability of a severe battle with the Arabs.

The Jewish volunteers who were present requested Einstein to stay but Einstein declined. He said that by doing so, he would become a prisoner and be deprived of his work and friends.

Before Einstein's lecture began, the organisers while introducing him said that two thousand years ago, Titus and his rival army faced each other at this spot. A temple of science was to come up there.

Einstein was quite influenced by all these incidents. He made his first statement in broken and improper Hebrew. Afterwards, he gave his lecture in French. In the end, he spoke German.

He toured Palestine during the next few days. He planted trees in the Mount Carmel Garden, outside of Haifa and visited a school and a technical institute in the area. He was satisfied by the work done and sent a letter to Weizmann about it. He also wrote that though some problems still existed yet the people were involved in the work. Soon education in higher classes would start.

When he was awarded honorary citizenship in a grand ceremony at Tel Aviv, he said that though he had got honorary citizenship of New York City, yet this honour made him ten times happier because he was receiving it from his own Jewish brothers. He repeated the vow and assured them of his support for establishing a new country for the Jews.

Einstein's love for the Jews was reflected in his suggestions. He said that in the last 2,000 years the Jews had given birth to brilliant children. The work of all those should be honourably registered. Despite being scattered all over the world, they had maintained their traditions. These traditions ought to be continued. Now the Jews were involved in building their own country. This country must also be the most unique one.

Einstein also appreciated the good things of the world. He said that he liked the dresses of Arab farmers. The life of the Japanese seemed acceptable to him. Almost everywhere, he appreciated the feasts organised by the Japanese in his honour. During his trip his violin remained with him and he usually played it for his host after the meal.

During the journey, strict security arrangements were made for him. Cannons were fired in his honour. Einstein felt uneasy with all these things. Elsa also did not like these formalities.

Einstein returned in the middle of February. The memories of the trip to Palestine were engrained in his mind. In his letter to Weizmann, he quite strongly expressed his desire to create a Jewish Nation. But his opinion was different regarding some matters. He wanted to make a clear-cut agreement with the Arab countries for the creation of a Jewish nation. Many respected Jews supported his suggestion. He said that the committees of the Jews should be created to talk to the Arab farmers and villagers. He was worried about the attitudes of the Arabs. Their attitudes were strict as regards this matter.

In 1925, the Hebrew University which was created for the Jews, started working in a formal way. But Einstein was unhappy with the attitude of Judah Magnesh, who was the administrator of the university. It seemed to him that he was working for the benefit of America, because it had invested a substantial amount of money in it.

The University was continuously expanding. Einstein was made a member of its Board of Governors. In September 1925, one of the meetings was held under his presidentship at Munich. Later, the strength of the board was increased. While the Academic Council was created, the Palestine Action Committee was also formed. Two controlling centres for this university were formed. One centre was in London where Weizmann had been appointed lifetime President of the University Board, and the second centre was at Jerusalem, where Judah Magnesh had been appointed Chancellor.

Magnesh was more influenced by the Jewish community of New York as he had resided there before World War I. His thoughts were also different from Weizmann's. Fortunately, Weizmann supported Magnesh during the decade 1925-35, while Einstein continued opposing him.

With the establishment of the University, contrary pulls also began. Einstein was quite vociferous. Most of the finances for the University were provided by the Americans and they were fond of Magnesh. Magnesh also had good experience in education. But his way of working was different. In 1925, a controversy broke out between Einstein and Magnesh. This controversy, which arose at a board meeting, slowly intensified.

Owing to this conflict, Weizmann came to Berlin to act as mediator. Einstein had decided to resign. Weizmann advised him, "If you resign, Magnesh will become all powerful." He also said that the University still worked on donations for which it was dependent on Magnesh. Since the University was fulfilling most of its responsibilities, controversy would make its existence impossible.

But Einstein was no longer able to tolerate Magnesh's arbitrariness. On June 14, 1928, he decided to abstain from matters related to the University. His Jewish friends and well-wishers suggested that he should not make it public. Also, Einstein had so much love for the University that he hesitated to do so.

In August 1929, the Sixteenth Jewish Congress was organised in Zurich. Einstein arrived there as he had to give a lecture and meet Mileva and his children. He bought a cigar from his old shop and had a long and pleasant conversation with his family.

The Jewish Movement had to face many obstacles. In Palestine, anti-Jewish riots started. A great preacher of Judaism died after his operation. At that time, the share market in America crashed and Europe came under the grip of the depression. The source of finance for the future Jewish nation dried up. It faced a great setback. Einstein was not directly affected but he was upset. Jewish leaders demanded severe punishment for the Arab killers of the Jews. But Einstein had a different view. He emphasised that more investigations should be done to look into the psychological aspects of these incidents. Instead of English, the Arabs should be taught in their own language.

Instead of provoking them, efforts should be made to normalise the atmosphere. He quoted Gandhi on his attitude of turning the other cheek to the offender.

However, Einstein became attached to Judaism. He always took the lead - from attending the mourning ceremonies of the Jews and playing music for peace to collecting funds for the welfare of their families.

□

Preparations for Migration

After recovering from his illness in 1928, Einstein started thinking that illness had its own benefits. A sick person gets sufficient time to think. Physically, Einstein became very weak; mentally, he became stronger.

After his recovery, he started contacting his friends in Germany and other European countries. He wrote letters to his American friends and also to his other well-wishers. He celebrated his fiftieth birthday that year.

He resumed his scientific activities once again. His aim was the theory of integration to which all other hypotheses are related. When he put up the proposal to other scientists, they felt that it was impossible. Wolfgang Pauli said that the combination of electromagnetic laws and gravitational laws was impossible.

On the other hand, scientists like Eddington were optimistic. Some of Einstein's research papers had already been published on this subject. It became a topic for debate in the newspapers. Many journalists had published his interviews in them. Even a great Austrian scholar like Dr.

Walther Mayer associated with him to work as his assistant on this subject. In October 1931, the theory of integration was published.

On the occasion of his fiftieth birthday, there was a grand celebration. Paris University, along with many other universities, honoured him by awarding him honorary doctorates. The Berlin administration accepted him in the aristocratic class of the city. As an honour to Einstein, it proposed that he should be presented a house and a garden.

Since Einstein was quite fond of boating, the house to be gifted to Einstein should have a river or a lake near it so that during his leisure time he might go for boating. Excited as Elsa was, she had already located a house with these facilities and had secretly inspected it.

The Berlin Council had a building of this type but it had already been given on lease. So, they selected an empty site near it. It was decided that Einstein should build a house there. He himself should bear the expenses. But there was an obstacle. The agreement in the previous lease was that no building should come up in this area. Now there was just one way out of it. Einstein's plot should remain empty.

The council proposed that Einstein could select a plot for himself and the council would pay for it. Elsa selected a site. When the proposal came up for the approval, one of the nationalist parties opposed it and questioned Einstein's eligibility. They even noted that he did not deserve to choose his gift.

It is quite evident that it had raised intense discussions and the decision on the proposal was postponed to the next meeting.

When Einstein became aware of the situation, he wrote a letter of thanks to the Mayor of the City. His birthday had become an old story and there was no need for any gift.

Einstein himself bought that plot and, later, built a house there. He became the owner of the house, though this process had cost him all his savings. Mockingly, Einstein said that now he had become a landlord and he felt safer.

The surroundings of the new house were like that of a village and more natural. Though the building was along the main road, yet it got crowded only at weekends when people visited the beautiful forests, lakes and waterfalls nearby.

The most interesting thing was that the architect who designed the building had done an astonishing job of blending nature with modernity. It was built mostly with wood.

Now Einstein's life seemed more organised. He studied and slept in the room on the top floor and the books were arranged in an orderly manner. One window opened towards the balcony and the beautiful scenery outside could be viewed from there. There was the desk where Einstein worked. His friends gifted him a boat on his next birthday.

Whenever Einstein highlighted the origin and development of the world on the basis of his Theory of Relativity, people would ask whether he believed in God or not.

Einstein would reply, "I believe in God who is responsible for the system which prevails in nature. I don't believe in God who keeps records of the destiny and deeds of man." Einstein also put forward his thoughts on religion and said it is the abnormality of the feelings and psychology of men. On the basis of this existence, nature should be believed. Its basis should be logical for everything.

He believed that religion should not be an obsession. His thoughts were inspired by humanism. He believed that science and religion influence different aspects of human life and they are not opposed to each other; on the contrary, they complement each other.

Einstein had become quite busy after coming to the new house. Lots of people and journalists used to visit his house. Since there was no telephone, people would come without an appointment to Potsdam by train and take the bus to his house. The visitors used to discuss different subjects like war and peace, the future of nuclear power, literature, etc. Otto Hahn, who had done research on the process of controlling nuclear fission, also had long discussions with him.

Gurudev Rabindranath Tagore, who had won the Nobel Prize for literature, also held discussions with him. Fortunately, when this discussion was published, Einstein felt outraged and said that when two people talked with trust, it would be wrong to make it public.

Einstein and Gurudev had discussion on love, beauty, etc. Gurudev said that if truth and beauty are separated from men, they would cease to have meaning. If the world is void of men, there would be no use for beauty. Einstein agreed that beauty is nothing without men, but he had different views about truth. He believed in the independent existence of truth. During the discussion, Einstein could not stop himself from claiming that he was more religious than his guest. He also tried to prove that scientific truths were not dependent on man. To prove his point, he spoke of Pythagoras' theorem and said that it being true was not related in any way with the existence of man. Even before man's existence, this theorem gave similar results. No reality was dependent on the existence of man. But it was also true that the truth which was beyond man's reach was very difficult to know and understand. This was the reason why truth was considered beyond the knowledge of man.

Our experiences and thoughts were such that several times the true meaning did not emerge.

Similar discussions occurred with other guests. Looking towards the sky many times he would say that they knew nothing about it. Over all, men knew very little of the world they lived in – like children in school. Shrugging his shoulders, he would say that even though we were trying to learn the mysteries like Socrates did, nothing much would come of it.

Within these discussions, Einstein continued to expound his integrated theory. This was the period of changes. On one side, quantum mechanics had taken shape. On other, a new telescope had been installed at California. Efforts were being made to have a closer look at the universe with its help. In the field of atomic physics, more and more information about the atom was being collected.

Einstein had one more specialty. He never needed any instrument for his work. During this period, there were no computers. He progressed just with the help of observations. Scientists from all over the world used to visit Einstein with their latest discoveries to discuss them with him. When the Russian scientist Abraham Joffe came to discuss the mechanical and electrical qualities of crystals, the discussion became so serious and long that they forgot about time. Dinner was served at 8 o'clock at night, but Einstein was so involved in the discussion that he was not able to eat his food properly with the help of a fork. Sometimes, the food used to fall down and at other times, the fork used to leave its mark on his face.

Somehow, dinner got over, but discussion continued. Joffe was already late for the last train to his city. It was midnight. When Joffe said that they could continue the discussion some other day, Einstein was so intensely involved in it that he did not hear.

Discussion stopped only when both were satisfied. Such incidents occurred with some other scientists also. He visited other scientists several times and disturbed their daily routine. Most of the time, he used to wake up early in the morning at 4 o'clock. He used to do his study and writings on the host's table and chair. He used to write on anything like bills and receipts that he got his hands to.

Once he wrote on the bill of Plesch's shoes. When Plesch asked him for the bill because he was to get a repayment, Einstein realised that the paper had now become valuable because a new equation had been written on it. So, he gave his recently acquired gold medal in exchange. The reason was that Einstein was getting many honours, medals, prizes and gifts.

But everything was not so good. The conflict between the nationalists and the peace lovers was intensifying in Germany. The peace lovers and the people all over the world were openly seeking support from Einstein and using him in several ways. All the work Einstein had done till then, his behaviour and his participation in several revolutions, were going against him.

There was one more reason why the tide was turning against him. Einstein mostly favoured Jewish students or foreigners. For the translations of his articles or for other work, he used to give them priority. These people, who were hated by the Germans, were benefitting most from their idol.

The situation in Germany was deteriorating. The influence of the Nazis was increasing. The shops of the Jews were being looted. The Jews were apprehensive about their future. Einstein also thought about it while sailing across the lake.

Many scientists were also organising themselves against Einstein. One hundred German scientists together published a book against his theory. Absurd remarks were made about the theory of relativity.

It seemed to Einstein that these problems were just a small part of bigger problems to come. He thought of finding a job and settling in some other country. He suggested that other Jews should also do so; initially, he was somewhat hesitant.

It was not that easy. Many physicists in Berlin loved him so much that it was not easy for him to oppose them. Furthermore, the employment of several people was dependent on him. He also had a feeling of gratitude to Germany. He had written letters several times to his friends advising them to leave the country or to apply for jobs at some other place, but he failed to post them.

Though he was giving his service to the educational institutes in several countries, he remained loyal to Kaiser Wilhelm Institute. California Institute of Technology asked for his regular services, while Christ Church, Oxford provided him with fellowships for his research.

During this period of turmoil, Einstein continued to fulfill his responsibilities to the different institutions. He even benefitted from this. His relations with the royal family of Belgium were cordial and he got to know that Germany was seeking to utilise the uranium there in developing nuclear weapons.

He had similar relations with the royal family of Britain. Queen Elizabeth, who was Princess Elizabeth at that time, invited him to play the violin and also accompanied him. The photographs taken at this occasion became the centre of attraction.

Einstein was invited for particular feasts on several occasions. At one feast at the British palace, there were just vegetarian items and there were no servants present. While at the feast, the host ate his favourite vegetables, potato and radish, he was looking for a piece of paper to note down the thoughts that had suddenly occurred to him, but he could not find a sheet of paper.

Einstein carried several things in his pocket like a knife attached with pen, pieces of rope, broken biscuits, small pieces of paper, old bus tickets, coins, partly burnt fragments of the tobacco taken out from the pipe, etc.

Several times, important papers used to come out of his pockets in a very bad condition. One could find in his pockets poems devoted to him by the royal family, important formulae, complex calculations, etc. Queen Victoria was his great fan, but Einstein was not able to handle the items presented by her.

Einstein was also spending a lot of time in formulating the relationship between religion and science. He wrote an article in the New York Times on this subject, in which he put before the world a different concept from the religious beliefs that were prevalent at that time. His thoughts were considered to be extraordinary for his time. Not only the media but also his friends and assistants were eager to hear his thoughts. He had no belief in the Church. He considered religious faiths to be mere foolishness. He also said that not believing in God was not wise. Since he had explained the mystery of inter-conversion of matter and energy to the world, he believed that someone must be behind such tremendous energy.

Einstein had an intelligent mind. He also believed that the human mind was too small and was unable to understand the reason for the harmony that existed in this world. He was quite angry with the people who were using his thoughts to deny the existence of God.

His articles relating to religion and science evoked wide-spread reaction. In his article that was published on the first page of the New York Times, he had written that man remained unable to reach his goals despite all his mental processes. He tried to abstain from sorrows or troubles. Religious beliefs had also developed in a fixed pattern. Common people adopted religion due to fear and tried to save themselves from evil. Later, religion made its way into the social fabric that controlled society. Slowly, the whole world revolved around religion.

He realised that religion had become the most powerful thing in the world. It had also encouraged scientific research.

Some people supported Einstein's thoughts on religion. These thoughts were different from the thoughts of the common man, but they had logic behind them. The Catholic priests declared his thoughts absurd.

Einstein continued advocating the shapeless inner spirit, universe following a fixed law, religion without church, detachment from wealth, protest against the increasing hold of materialism, an international government, democracy etc. These beliefs invited opposition from many quarters.

Einstein got several proposals to work as a commercial model. The manufacturers of musical instruments, beauty products, clothes, etc. were eager for one single statement. They all wanted him to just say that he had used their products and was satisfied with them.

But Einstein considered these proposals an insult. He wanted to limit his use for peace and Judaism. As a result, several people became angry with him.

Despite all this confusion, Einstein continued his travels, but he was not able to avoid displeasure. The company on whose ship he travelled used to be happy, but the fellow travellers used to get angry and upset with him.

When he got down from a ship, a group of fifty people surrounded him. They bombarded him with several questions on science, politics, religion, etc. Questions were also asked about his violin.

An officer of the German Embassy and Elsa helped a lot to answer the questions that were asked in different languages. Einstein even joked in between, but the questions of the journalists were getting serious. Every question was a subject of total discussion. He was asked about Hitler. Einstein replied that he was aware of Hitler as he was the person ruling over the empty stomachs of the people. As soon as the economic condition of Germany improved, his importance would diminish.

Einstein did not hesitate to help the poor people. He broadcast his speech for radio companies from the ship and used to distribute his earnings to the poor people of Berlin. While on his voyage on a ship, he broadcast for two radio companies and donated 1,000 dollars earned from them.

Artists were always eager to sketch Einstein's portrait. Normally, Einstein disliked such exposure. So, they were always on the lookout for an opportunity. One day, when he was eating food in the dining hall of a ship, an artist who sat beside him secretly sketched him. When Einstein finished eating, the artist showed him his creation. Einstein laughed heartily. After some hesitation, he put his signature on it and wrote: 'This fat pig-like person looks like Einstein."

People were eager to get his autograph. It, too, was not to his liking. He found a way out. He established a fund for the poor people of Berlin and started to charge three dollars for a normal autograph and five dollars for an autograph over a photograph. Elsa kept the accounts and duly disbursed the fund.

When the ship to New York halted at Havana, Einstein saw that there were clubs full of leisure loving people on one side. On the other side, there was severe poverty. Einstein developed a deep sympathy for the blacks there.

Einstein was steadily becoming popular in America. Crowds would throng around him for his autograph. Einstein would laughingly remark that his business was running well. Perhaps, there would be no more poor people in Berlin.

He took time out for his scientific work also. During this time, Hubble and Humason telescopes were set up in an observatory. On the basis of their observations, the scientists assumed that the universe was not stable. But everyone had a different view on the methods to prove it. Earlier, it was believed that the Milky Way, which has the sun and similar stars, was the universe. There was no doubt about it. Now it was clearly evident that the dim light was coming from some other galaxy. Scientists realised that there were stars which were at a distance of approximately 8 lakh light years away. This distance is eight times more than the distance of the most distant star of our Milky Way.

The new discoveries created a sensation in the scientific world. The blooming universe was called Einstein's world. Plenty had been imagined regarding the origin of the universe and of the Big Bang. It was believed that the expansion of the universe might have started about 1,000 crore years after the great explosion.

Two months had elapsed and Einstein was so involved in these new discoveries that he was hardly aware of the passing time. Some of his explanations astonished not only the students but also the teachers. He not only talked about scientific facts but also about other things—how people kill one another in wars, how during peace people become slaves of machines. On the one hand, he kept meeting peace-makers. On the other, he went on participating in those programmes for raising funds for the Jews. Before he could get on the ship, a group of peace-makers arrived with a banner to meet him. He gave them the message that they should not serve in the army at all. This was what would lead them to success.

He had to leave for England from Berlin as Oxford University was awarding him with an honorary doctorate. He was given a formal welcome as he reached Oxford. There, he met many families of the scientists as well as visited many places. He vividly described the Theory of Relativity.

He made the audiences aware of the difficulties that might come up in proving his hypotheses. On the request of the audiences, he gave speeches in English. He revealed the obstacles he came across in proving his laws. People were surprised to know about the way the universe expanded. They could not believe the estimated age of the world.

When Lindemann, Einstein's host in England, came to know about Nazi atrocities and the suppression of the Jews in Germany, he invited him to come to Oxford and suggested that he should reside there permanently. He could fulfill his responsibilities at Berlin. Lindemann told him that he would receive a fellowship of 400 pounds per year.

He could reside in the college hostel and arrangements would be made for his food. Considering the situation, Einstein accepted the offer. During this period, the rights of the parliament of Germany were withdrawn and there was great unrest. At the same time, he received an invitation from America. In this proposal, which was given in the latter half of 1931, there was a remuneration of 5,000 dollars. The most interesting thing was that the American scientists were so eager to have Einstein that they proposed a ridiculously high salary. Einstein asked them to reduce it.

Later he changed his mind regarding leaving Germany and informed the Americans about it. But he went to America for a short-term programme. He gave lectures on the subject like the obliqueness of the universe or elliptical shape of the universe.

In May 1932, he went to England and gave lectures at Oxford and Cambridge. He realised that an atmosphere of dirty politics hung over Oxford and it was not that advanced in the sciences as it should have been. The situation in Germany was changing rapidly. The country was under the rule of paramilitary forces. People were terrified also. Einstein did not fear much but his foreign friends were very apprehensive. Princeton University in America sent an invitation to him. Einstein was given the right to fix his salary. He said that an amount of 3,000 dollars annually was sufficient for him.

In reply, the American scientist Flexner wrote that it was not enough. He also wrote that Einstein should not worry about the salary. Mrs Einstein and he together would fix his salary. At last, a salary of 16,000 dollars per annum was fixed and he was given a proposal of lifelong employment. Now, the Einstein couple was in a dilemma.

The Hebrew University had been trying its best to soothe Einstein's anger. Though detailed information was not known about the decision taken during the long discussions between Mackienzy and Weizmann, yet Weizmann wrote to Einstein, saying that all his complaints, problem or grievances would be redressed and he should come and take responsibility of the Board of the University.

Einstein accepted Weizmann's proposal without any investigation and he immediately gave advice to the Physics Department. This shows the depth of his attachment to the university.

Friends of Einstein, i.e. Lindemann, Flexner, etc. believed that Einstein would have to leave Germany. So, they made arrangements for his stay. In the meanwhile, the number of his opponents in America had increased. An organisation passed a proposal that Einstein's views regarding peace were strange and off-balance. His scientific theories did not have any scientific value or aim. His theories could not even be understood. People also started to believe that he was a socialist. One organisation of women demanded a ban on his visa.

Einstein was amused at this opposition from the women. But he became more alert. He continued his opposition to war. When a proposal came to him from the politburo of the Socialist Soviet union, he refused to sign it.

Einstein clarified that he considered Lenin a great leader, but did not like the struggle for power that was going on in the Soviet Union. Many people wanted Russian power to be utilised for the protection of the Jews in Germany. But it seemed to Einstein that it was not a good idea to take the support of one evil power to suppress another evil force.

At last, he received the American visa. He went by train to Antwerp and continued his journey by ship. Before leaving his house, he told Elsa with tears in his eyes to take a last loving look at their house. Perhaps, they would not get a chance to see it again.

He reached California in January 1933. He had visited California very often in the past but this time the situation appeared changed. Though his connection with Germany had not formally ended, yet he accepted the fact that he might have to remain in America.

On reaching America, he received a grant of 7,000 dollars on the condition that he would try to improve relations between Germany and America. His American friends feared his habits, thoughts and his statements. His opponents were also becoming strong. One army officer said that the Americans just gave one lakh dollars to Madame

Curie to buy radium. The cost was ten lakh dollars in the eyes of Einstein for the same radium. Investing an amount blindly on Einstein was a sign of destruction.

Einstein's friends stood up in his defence. They said that each and every person had made use of Einstein. From great scientists to Charlie Chaplin, they all had taken his support. His thoughts were always of the highest quality. It depended entirely on the Americans to decide how they could use Einstein for their benefit.

□

New Circumstances

As soon as Einstein reached America on January 23, his speech about American-German relations was broadcast over the radio. He had decided that he would avoid talking to strangers. Despite this, he made many new friends.

Strangers, who were supporters of peace, started to meet him and suggested to use his name and influence for their purpose. Those who were working for the establishment of a Jewish nation were also pulling him towards them. Einstein made it clear that he would not return to Germany. But the news of his activities reached Germany. The Jews were migrating from Germany. Some even migrated to America. With great hope they used to come to meet Einstein. Einstein used to play the violin for them and console them.

There developed hatred against him in Germany. An office of a Jewish organisation was raided. The street which was named after Einstein eleven years ago was renamed. The sign bearing Einstein's name was removed. Sixteen hundred Jewish teachers were dismissed from the university. The books which had been translated into Hebrew were burnt to ashes.

Einstein's house was raided. The reason given was that the authorities were suspicious of weapons hidden there. The police were under the influence of the workers of the Nazi Party. During that time, Einstein was on a trip in Europe.

Over all, Einstein's life was at its low ebb. He was annoyed by the expulsion of the Jews from Germany. Hitler was gaining his supreme position. Einstein's relations with Hebrew University were not improving. He was not able to understand clearly what he should do.

He, finally, decided to relinquish his German citizenship. He went to the German Embassy and gave up his German rights. Due to lack of formalities, there were some drawbacks.

In Germany the situation was becoming worse. Berlin was always a cosmopolitan city. But the Nazis destroyed this. They burnt books and documents of the Germans like Einstein, Faraday, Thomas Mann and of the Americans like Helen Keller. Forty thousand residents of Berlin not only witnessed these acts but encouraged the rioters. In this conflagration, about 2,000 rare books and documents were burnt to ashes. People cheered having seen the rising flames.

German University underwent a drastic change. Nationalism and fascist politics reared heads. Between April 4 to May 15, 16 11 German professors had either resigned or were dismissed. A list of people who opposed the Nazis was published. Their bank accounts were sealed. Dr. Plesch, who used to host Einstein, had to flee Germany.

Einstein continued to travel and give lectures in other universities of Europe. Many Jewish scholars made a proposal to meet him and work with him. Einstein proposed to establish a University for Jewish refugees in England. But he was unable to give sufficient time to it. Nor did he receive sufficient support.

People had many expectations from Einstein. So, he had to face several criticisms. Someone said, "People who are very intelligent are usually more impractical."

They were also upset about his feeling of disenchantment with Hebrew University. They felt that Einstein could have got help for Jewish students and teachers from there.

Einstein was also thinking in an innovative way under these changing circumstances. Weizmann was trying his best to reconnect Einstein with Hebrew University. He was upset with Magnesh and believed that Einstein had been humiliated by him. It was a loss to the Jewish community also.

Hitler wanted to drive out the Jews. Some had migrated to France, Austria and Czechoslovakia. Everyone was worried. Weizmann planned to move some people out to Jerusalem for the benefit of the Jews. Proposals were also made to establish another institute for the Jews.

At last, people started realising the truth in Einstein's words. News poured in from Jerusalem about the irregularities in the administration of the university. Einstein was being pressurised that, instead of keeping away from Hebrew University, he should pay more attention to its activities. But Einstein specified that though Hebrew University was important for him, yet Physics was equally important. During this period, he and Flexner were involved in an important work and he did not want to leave it.

Einstein openly criticised some activities of Hebrew University. That was why some people turned against him. But many people wanted a proper investigation into the irregularities of the university.

At the end of 1933 an enquiry team was formed which toured Jerusalem. This team did a thorough investigation and recommended several vital changes. Though no immediate action was taken about these recommendations, yet on September 23, 1935, Einstein was duly informed about them and was told that Magnesh had been removed from the executive post and appointed to a temporary one. In his place, Prof. Bormann, who had early worked with Einstein, was given the responsibility.

Now Einstein regained hope that the university would be capable of attracting young scholars. Magnesh was appointed president. The post was equivalent to the post of Chancellor in a British University. He continued to maintain good co-ordination with the British Government. But he was anguished that Einstein was the cause of his lower status. He believed that, due to Einstein, the university was not able to do justice to the Jewish students settled in Germany during the period of crisis. But several people appreciated Einstein's obstinate and vociferous nature. According to them, his most powerful weapon was his honesty.

While there was turmoil in Hebrew University, conditions for the next world war were being created in Europe. Einstein was the only hope of the pacifists.

Discussions were carried out for disarmament while a proposal was forwarded for the creation of an armed international police with emphasis on making it effective. Everyone wanted to harness Einstein's support for their side.

Einstein's thinking was also changing. He also felt that letting people abstain from the army was not only impractical but it did not make any contribution to peace also.

Those people, who were defying the government order to serve in the army, were being put in jail. It seemed to the well-wishers of Einstein that he would be abducted or murdered. During his tour of Europe, Einstein often went to Belgium. The place where he stayed was a three hour journey from the German border.

Many European universities asked Einstein to join them permanently. Many people sympathised with him because he had no house and that there was a serious threat to his life.

Their apprehensions were not baseless. The people, affected by German fascism, were uniting together on a single platform. On the other side were the scholars and the philosophers who were trying to flee from Germany, were captured and were brought back by the Nazis. Several of them were killed. One German Nationalist Organisation issued a contract to kill Einstein and announced that the killer would get 5,000 dollars as reward. But Einstein did not get distraught. He even said that the one who would kill him should keep his plans secret. People were worried and the police in Belgium were tormented by the threat. But Einstein was carefree. The police were increasing their security ring around Einstein but he always used to move out of it.

When he reached England, strict security arrangements were made for him. It was suggested that if any stranger tried to come near him, he should be apprehended immediately. Despite all these arrangements, a photographer managed to come close to him and he took snaps of his sweater, sandals, etc.

His step son-in-law, Dmitri, continued to send his articles on the Theory of Relativity to the French newspapers. One renowned Jewish artist was making his portrait. On the artist's request, he sat comfortably leaning against the open door. In between, he cracked jokes and sometimes played the piano and the violin. To lighten the atmosphere, he, now and then, released smoke from his pipe.

Hitler's influence over Germany was increasing and a civil war had started in Spain. Britain was badly entangled at every front.

Einstein got news about Haber. Despite being a Jew, he believed in Christian ideology. Even then, he was not spared in Germany. He was forced to resign from Kaiser Wilhelm Institute. He was even denied a pension. Haber was full of sorrow. In his farewell letter, Einstein wrote that he was feeling very sad to leave this institute after twenty-two years of service.

Haber was the only person who had suggested to Einstein in 1921 to keep away from the Jewish movement. Homeless as Haber was, he wanted to go to Jerusalem. But there were several problems. Weizmann wanted experienced renowned learned people like Haber to go to Jerusalem but Einstein was in favour of young people in Jerusalem.

Haber felt quite offended. He came to England, but he was not happy in Cambridge. Some people even said that if Haber was invited, they would not attend the university. Many people did not want to even shake hands with Haber, the inventor of chemical weapons, because these weapons were used against the British.

Haber went to Switzerland, but he returned availing himself of an opportunity to meet Weizmann. Weizmann suggested that he should go to Palestine and said that the atmosphere there was suitable for him. There, he would get good laboratories and assistants; he would get peace and honour and a homely atmosphere. Haber happily got ready to go there.

Einstein's opponents had united in England. On October 3, when Einstein was on his way to present a lecture, a large crowd had gathered to hear him. The hall with a capacity of 10,000 people was full and many people were even standing. Just then, the news came that there was a plot hatched by the Nazi supporters in London to murder Einstein.

The most remarkable thing took place. As soon as the police were informed, they made full security arrangements.

Above all, about 1,000 students of London University formed a defence ring around Einstein and helped the police in the operation.

At this meeting, Einstein was quite enthusiastic and he gave his lecture in English. He spoke not only in favour of the Jews but also in favour of those who suffered owing to their acquaintance with the Jews. Without even mentioning the name of Germany, he said that peace could not be achieved just with rules.

Einstein's personality acted like a magnet at that conference. He had a glow on his face. Like a well-versed artist, he expressed his feelings in different ways. The outcome of this conference was that sufficient finance for the education of the refugees affected by the turmoil in Germany was collected. Many universities came forward to help.

But confusion still prevailed. The British thought Communist Russia was an upcoming power and that a powerful Germany would work as a shield to overpower it. Many people even believed that if commercial, political and traditional relations with Germany prevailed, a war could be avoided.

Einstein had to give one more lecture, but arrangements could not be made for it. On October 7, 1933, he planned to return to America. He said that he was going there just for six months and he would return to Oxford in the summer of 1934. Perhaps, he hoped to get an offer of British citizenship.

When he reached New York, a grand reception was organised and he was taken to Princeton. There, a house was rented for his accommodation. He continued his work as a research scholar. But Einstein still had a strange attraction for Europe. He still remembered the intellectual environment of Berlin. He recalled the discussions with Bohr at Copenhagen, the evenings spent in London, Zurich and Oxford. He remembered Rutherford and Thomson as well. He also knew that a bill to grant him citizenship was under consideration in the British House of Commons.

The atmosphere was totally different at Princeton. It was green everywhere. The classes were not conducted at graduation level and there were no arrangements for games. Many scholars who fled from Germany became Einstein's friend within no time. His intellectual meetings started with them.

Einstein and Elsa continued to live nearby in a rented house. He had very little work, i.e. teaching. Soon, he became popular. A German scholar came to the US after fleeing Germany and had difficulty telling the address of his destination to the immigration officers. But they immediately guessed and said that it seemed that he wanted to go to Einstein's Institute and they sent him there.

We can guess about his popularity by the fact that a small girl used to come to him in order to get her mathematical problems solved. Bus drivers also knew him because he often made mistakes in counting money.

Einstein became popular as an absent-minded and disorderly person. Some people used to laugh at him. Some people sympathised with him and said that he utilised his time in useful things. He was not a slave of material things like bathrooms, cars, radios, etc. People close to him noticed that he seldom visited the barber. His hair was long and unkept. He did not feel the need for socks. He had a leather jacket which also served as a coat. He used to pay attention to his shirt, trousers, jacket and shoes, only when he went out or gave lectures. He even said that without them it would not be appropriate.

Elsa was also gaining popularity. She mixed with the high society, but she abstained from pomp and show.

In November, President Roosevelt's secretary telephoned and arranged for his meeting with Roosevelt at dinner at the White House. There, a controversy arose. Due to unknown reasons, Flexner who had brought Einstein to the US objected and called Roosevelt's secretary to say that it was not appropriate. He wrote a letter to the President and informed him that Einstein was doing scientific work in solitude and his participation in social activities was not right.

In reality, Flexner felt bad that Einstein had accepted the invitation without consulting him. On the contrary, he argued that New York had an irresponsible group of Nazi supporters. If Einstein participated in social activities, it would not only hamper his work but endanger his life also.

There was not a bit of truth in Flexner's logic. Einstein had not only participated in the dinner organised by Governor Lehman but had also played the violin there. He had already participated in an all-people conference of a Jewish newspaper. Fear of Nazi groups was just an excuse. Flexner knew that President Roosevelt would be impressed by Einstein and would ask him to use his capabilities and energy for the benefit of America. Flexner's views had an effect on Einstein. So, he declined the invitation. But he had a doubt. Einstein understood that Flexner was quite different from what he had thought him to be till then. Roosevelt felt that Einstein had refused because his office had not invited him in a proper and respectful way.

As both the sides had an urge to meet, another invitation came from the White House. On January 24, the families of Einstein and Roosevelt had dinner together. After dinner, they had a long discussion on important matters. Both spoke in German and Einstein was quite astonished to see that Roosevelt had a good command of the German language.

Late at night, it was decided that Einstein would spend the night there. The views that Einstein expressed on the occasion are still preserved in the White House.

The matter of Einstein's citizenship was still unsolved. Roosevelt was advised to grant citizenship to Prof. Einstein by an official order. Roosevelt himself wanted to do this, but his secretary cautioned him that the American Congress would not appreciate it. However, the Labour Secretary was instructed to look into this matter and make arrangements. Einstein had Swiss citizenship and he was living in America on a temporary visa.

On March 28, a proposal was made to grant American citizenship to Einstein. Fortunately, the very next day, by an order, all his rights in Germany were abolished. Several people met with the similar fate. Though Einstein did not react, yet he was deeply hurt. After many years he made a statement that he had relinquished his German rights long before. He said, "I had a fate similar to Mussolini who was hanged despite the fact that he was already dead."

Though he was quite happy with his Swiss citizenship, yet he accepted the American citizenship with honour. After gaining citizenship, his activities increased. He started to participate openly in the activities of Jewish Organisations. He was frequently getting invitations from Oxford, but Einstein felt that the situation in America was quite favourable. In America, several universities were attempting to attract him.

That was a good thing. Had Einstein gone to Europe, he would have become the centre of Hitler's opposition. Secondly, he would have been more in contact with the members of his family and would give less time to scientific work. Mileva and both the children were safe in Switzerland. His eldest step-daughter, Elsay, had settled in Holland. The second daughter Margot was in Belgium. All his relatives who were scattered in Europe had settled on the other side of the Atlantic.

The Einstein couple searched for another house, a short distance away from Princeton. He wanted to reorganise his life.

Einstein started to invest more time in welfare programmes as numerous Jewish refugees were coming from Europe. Einstein met a radiologist, Dr. Watters. Soon they became good friends. Watters had one more specialty. He used to note down events related to Einstein's life. Both would often eat together and go for walks. Watters also treated the Jews. Since he was a good medical practitioner, he had a good image. He was also a good inventor. So, he corresponded frequently with Einstein. Soon, he became aware of Einstein's habits.

When Einstein had come to America, he remembered his old boat in Berlin. He used to sail in the 17-foot-boat. Many times, despite being tired and ill, he did not miss an opportunity to sail.

The remarkable thing about Einstein was that he had never driven a car but he used to navigate the boat quite skill-fully. He had such confidence in rowing that he never took a life jacket or belt with him.

Einstein hated machines. He wanted to be away from any sound of motor or machine. After he had turned fifty years old, he touched a camera for the first time. Though he was scared, yet, with great difficulty, he learned to use a typewriter.

Einstein was also afraid of speed. He was never interested to make or break a record. He did not like competition. His behaviour with the other scientists of his time was friendly. His likes and dislikes were childlike. He would be happy whether the boat moved or stopped.

Sometimes, he had the desire to go skiing. But he did not have sufficient facilities for it. One reason was that he was quite lazy by nature. He used to row the boat happily and move far off. He never kept a compass in his boat. He had premonition about the change of weather and storms. Perhaps, the reason was that the air, weather, etc. cause pressure on the body that lead to its actions and reactions. It was a part of Einstein's subject.

People were also impressed by these qualities. A designer named Bargesh had a long discussion with him on the best design from different models. After listening to him, Einstein took a paper and pencil and wrote down the formula and equation for a yacht on a piece of paper. After thinking for a few minutes, he gave his suggestions.

Many of his friends talked about his interest in a boat. People used to get surprised. Einstein did not fear even death while rowing a boat. Many times, he went sailing in bad weather. Apart from this, he also enjoyed the unimaginable incidents. Because of strong currents and high waves, the boat used to get unbalanced several times; people started to shout with fear but Einstein did not. He kept the boat balanced. At such times, he used to laugh as if he had been a child. Quite often, his boat narrowly escaped hitting submerged rocks.

In the prevailing condition of turmoil in Europe, before World War II, Einstein had to face trouble from his family. His elder step son-in-law, Rudolf Caesar, had to leave Germany after the Nazi uprising. He first went to Holland. Somehow, keeping himself safe, he reached Einstein at Princeton. His second step-daughter, Margot, also fled along with her husband and reached him. Later, both divorced.

Both of Einstein's sons were also in trouble. His second son fell victim to a fatal disease, which did not have any cure at that time. His elder son, Hans, was quite affected by his brother's illness. He left his mother in Zurich and moved to several places in search of a cure for his brother's disease.

Some months before World War II, Albert Einstein's sister, Maja, also fled from Italy and reached America. During that time, Albert Einstein had kept an extended and a regular correspondence with his relatives in Europe.

The Jews were fleeing Austria and Czechoslovakia also. Einstein had sympathy with the Jews who crossed the Atlantic leaving their homeland, property, etc. He helped them in all possible ways. These activities were badly affecting his research work. But he did not care. Openly and secretly, he was collecting funds for this purpose.

During that period, he did not want to waste a single moment. Many of his friends were giving him different suggestions but he did not heed them. His health was also weak. He felt the utmost necessity to visit England and Palestine but was unable to do so.

He regretted that because of the controversy with Magnesh he was not able to work for Hebrew University as much as was required. It was due to him that Magnesh was removed. Now, he needed to put in more effort, but he was not able to do so. He was also dreaming about the future Israel.

His activities and the atmosphere were attracting criticism for him in America. He had become habituated to opposition. Several theories along with his Theory of Relativity were called theories of the Jews. The opposition was now gaining a new dimension. Sometimes, his theory of physics was called German Physics and sometimes Aryan Physics.

Despite lack of time, Einstein was able to defend himself. He said, "Science is always for the whole world and nothing is part of science except the truth. It is always above any religion or community. An unending battle against fabrication continues regularly in science. It does not get affected by feelings or the madness of a few people."

Einstein's old associates, the German scientists, had also got scattered prior to World War II. Max Born had refused to work in Hitler's nuclear weapon programme. He fled to Cambridge first and then moved to Edinburgh. Another associate of Einstein, Otto Stern declined to accept Hitler as the ruler and resigned from his post. His staff did their best to make him understand, but he did not agree to their views. Suddenly, he disappeared. Later, he reached America. His other associate, Irwin Frederick, reached Istanbul and made a brave but unsuccessful attempt to establish a Western Centre of Education. Later, he went to Prague. From there, he reached Scotland and worked there for the rest of his life.

Schrödinger fled to Oxford. From there, he went to Belgium. Afterwards, he moved to Dublin. As soon as Hitler became Chancellor, Leo Szilard also reached England via Austria. When he did not get support there, he crossed the Atlantic and reached America. Six Nobel Laureates from Germany fled to America. America gave shelter to these scientists and recruited them in several important scientific projects.

The situation in Palestine was also changing before World War II. A reputed research institute sent frequent invitations to him. It was not possible for Einstein to go there in the prevailing circumstances in the sixth decade of his life. Everybody was worried about his health. Elsa herself was not keeping well. But she took great care of Einstein.

Once a person came to invite Einstein. Elsa gave him several instructions. She said clearly that he was not permitted to smoke cigars. He could have coffee at breakfast, but special care should be taken about his dinner; otherwise, he would not be able to sleep at night and he would get ill.

Now Einstein followed Elsa's instructions. That day after dinner, he smoked a pipe instead of a cigar. A few moments later, when someone offered him a cigar, he took it.

People associated with various fields visited Einstein and he was happy to show them his work. One person was working on a heart transplant which was a surprise during that period. Einstein had nothing to do with it. He saw his work and encouraged him.

By 1935, he had accepted that he could never re-establish himself in Europe. He had a desire to visit Europe and stay there. He visited Belgium in February 1935. Afterwards, he completed some formalities regarding the visa and came back to Princeton. During that period he kept himself away from reporters.

He decided to stay in America. He bought a double-storey house at 112, Mercer Street. Elsa liked the house very much because it had a beautiful garden. It was surrounded by trees and had a boundary of shrubs and hedges.

After buying it, some changes were made according to the needs of the Einstein couple. A study was made for him on the second floor. A big window was built there so that he might see the view. Long cupboards were made for the books. A set of papers, pencils, pipes etc. were provided. His table was in front of the window. Pictures of Faraday, Maxwell and later, Mahatma Gandhi, were fixed on the walls.

A notable point is that Einstein considered only Mahatma Gandhi as an international political leader and looked up to him with respect.

His diploma certificate was also hung on the wall. Fortunately, the Nazis had removed the furniture from his house in Germany and had sent it to America. Einstein kept it on the ground floor. He did not even look at it. Slowly, he started liking Princeton and started to appreciate it in his letters to his friends. In his letter to the Queen of Belgium, he wrote, "This place is beautiful and natural. Here, I am also getting enough freedom."

It appeared to the inhabitants of Princeton that Einstein was unhappy. Several people were apprehensive about his political thoughts and beliefs and several others felt irritated at his religious thoughts. But everyone agreed that he was a great person and encouraged their children to meet him. Despite being tired, Einstein never hesitated to meet his friends or neighbours. He wrote:

Sorrows and happiness are part of life.

This is the only truth of life.

Einstein never got enough happiness in his life. During that period, Elsa fell victim to a complicated disease. Elsa's eyes became swollen. Doctors believed it was due to some abnormalities that had occurred in the heart and the liver. They suggested he should take her to a hospital in New York for further treatment.

Elsa was more worried about Einstein than her disease. She felt that it was causing a lot of trouble to his work. Elsa, who understood Einstein's feelings, started to say that Albert was not able to sleep well due to her illness. His work which related to science, political movements, arts, etc. was at a low ebb.

Einstein found household responsibilities more complex than the theory of the origin of the universe. He had spent a decade with his first wife but his mind remained troubled. He had spent two decades with Elsa but was still troubled.

Elsa thought Einstein was an unusual person who was trying to discover how God created the world. Both felt worried about each other and ended up fighting several times.

Fortunately, Elsa regained her health by the summer of 1936. Now Einstein returned to his work and Elsa was satisfied with the honours he was getting. She never complained that he was not fulfilling his duties as a husband. At one stage, they took some time off and went on a vacation.

When they returned, Elsa's health deteriorated again. Einstein stopped his visits to Princeton Institute and made several rounds of the hospital. During these years, one of Elsa's daughters had died in Paris.

She was not able to bear the pain of the disease again. She left the world on December 21, 1936.

Now Einstein was all alone. In the beginning of 1937, he had become totally introverted. When his friends invited him to break his loneliness, he declined.

He became philosophical. Sometimes, he used to say that man is not born just to enjoy luxuries. He devoted himself entirely to scientific work, peace movements and care of the Jews. He felt that he had achieved great success in the creation of Hebrew University, but it had also cost him very dearly. He hoped to give many more universities to this world.

He returned to reality and started to work in his office at Princeton. He took time off for rowing. People close to him would ask, "Is this man really of this world?" Some people jokingly called him 'fossil'.

In Princeton, his assistants and associates were very influenced by his personality. They believed that if the problems of physics were put into his mind, they would melt and come out as answers from his mouth. People used to compare his writings with special treatises. They said that he was not only the best physicist but also a philosopher and a scholar of history.

A few months after the death of Elsa, it was his fifty-eighth birthday. According to the rules, he had to retire from his work. After reaching this stage, most scientists leave science and take up administrative roles, but Einstein continued with his research work.

People were astonished to see his work and used to raise several questions. Once his accountant asked him if he was close to his aim. Einstein immediately answered, "God never tells us beforehand that the path we have chosen is the only truth. We adopt ninety-nine ways and become unsuccessful. This only proves that the ninety-nine ways we had chosen were not right."

He was working on the integration of Theory of Relativity and the theory of the origin and development of the universe at the same time. A decade ago, he worked on the quantum theory also. He wanted young and intelligent boys and girls to give him fresh ideas and help him in his work. Till 1940, Princeton Institute was a part of the University. Usually in the seminars, he used to sit silently and observe how the students were using his theories and formulae. He used to speak in between and he had become a good speaker. His formula of E = mc2 was getting popular and the conversion of matter into energy was being measured in several ways. Einstein wanted to take physics closer to the common people. With this objective, he wrote a book called Origin of Physics with Leopold Enfield. Leopold had come to America after fleeing from Poland. In this book, the natural world, relativity, the development of the quantum theory, etc. are described in a simple style. It was very successful.

□

Creation of the Atom Bomb

By March 1938, Einstein had reached the zenith of his scientific works. Austria was attacked by Germany from one side and Italy from the other side.

People were still not quite clear of the situation when Czechoslovakia was overrun. Now Einstein adopted a new different stand and declared that it was impossible to fight dictators by preaching peace.

Owing to the German attack, a situation of chaos was created among the Jews of Austria. Einstein became restless. His sixtieth birthday passed without being noticed. He repented that he had become old and could not work according to the situation prevalent.

Despite this, he continued to help Jewish refugees. His sister, Maja, also required his help. Mussolini's atrocities in Italy were on the increase.

All the work done by Einstein till then was mostly theoretical. He had achieved great success. Under the new circumstances, he was not feeling happy. When Germany captured Poland, Einstein got news that his old associate

Otto Hahn had achieved success in breaking the mystery of atomic uranium.

The world took Otto Hahn's success lightly, but Einstein saw the danger of destruction inherent in it. J.J. Thomson, Planck, Rutherford, Niels Bohr and Einstein were the only people who, like Veda Vyasa, the great sage, had premonition of danger. Einstein had tested and seen the capabilities of Otto Hahn at the Kaiser Wilhelm Institute.

This nuclear fission generated a tremendous amount of energy. Destructive weapons could be manufactured using this energy. So, discussions on the topic increased. Bohr reached America and had discussions with other scientists. Madame Curie's daughter and son-in-law were also involved in this work.

Now the world had reached the stage of atomic war. On the request of scientists like Szilard and Fermi, the Dean of Columbia University wrote a letter to the Admiral of the American Navy, Hooper, in which he expressed his alarm about the probable danger of the nuclear weapon. He wrote that the weapon would be one crore times powerful and destructive than ordinary bombs.

Similar efforts were in progress not only in Germany, but in other countries also. Five atomic energy patents had been obtained in France. Out of these, one concerned the manufacture of the atom bomb. In Holland, on the request of physicists, the finance minister had given permission to purchase fifty tons of uranium. In Britain, efforts to develop nuclear weapons were in progress at the official level and the foreign ministry and the finance ministry were working in co-ordination. Efforts were being made to keep the uranium available in the world, out of Germany's hands. During this period, the only source of uranium was Congo, which was in the possession of Belgium.

Efforts were also in progress in Germany. One of Otto Hahn's assistants had prepared a research paper on the items which could be prepared from uranium. There were discussions about the mistakes that could occur in developing a nuclear weapon. Germany's war department also was quite vigilant about it. Germany was making all preparations for atomic war.

Einstein sensed all the developments and it did not take him long to understand the whole concept. It was as though Meghnad had hidden himself to perform the yagna of Nekumbhala Devi during the Rama-Ravana war. Vibhishan had already understood the ultimate result of the yagna.

Einstein wrote a letter, giving all the information and a summary of these incidents and their long-lasting effects, to the then American President, Roosevelt. What an irony! This was the same Einstein who was so upset by the destruction caused by World War I and had encouraged people to abstain themselves from the army and not to contribute or help in any way.

The same Einstein was encouraging the American administration to take the weapon into their hands which, later, took the lives of one lakh twenty thousand men, women and children, in just a few seconds.

Roosevelt also did not take much time to analyse the situation. Quick action was taken in compliance with Einstein's letter. The famous Manhattan Project was started. Many scientists along with Szilard got involved in the study and uses of the uranium chain reaction. Political action was like a double-sided sword. On one side, efforts were being made to develop the nuclear bomb and on the other side, efforts were being made to prevent Germany from laying hands on the stock of uranium.

Szilard got a secret letter from Einstein and carried it to the rulers in London, recommending the creation of obstacles to prevent Germany from obtaining uranium.

Einstein was in a dilemma. He was apprehensive about the military use of this powerful source of energy. He also did not want to leave his work regarding the theory of integration in an unfinished stage.

Uranium-238 is quite abundant in nature. For the process of nuclear fission, Uranium-235 is required and it is very difficult to extract it in its pure form. Scientists along with the friends of Einstein put their heads together to overcome this problem.

All of them were eager to involve Einstein in this project. Since Einstein had taken the first step, he gave indirect support right from the beginning. He also warned the American Government that the useful uranium was scarce in America but, along with Congo which was in the possession of Belgium, Canada and Czechoslovakia had a good stock. He recommended adequate finance for the experiment which was needed urgently.

Germany ordered a ban on the export of uranium from Czechoslovakia. In the US, more meetings and discussions were organised but very little was followed up practically. A ban was imposed over the publication of experiments on this subject. Szilard and Einstein pressurised the government to take the nuclear bomb project seriously or allow the research to be published. They opined that the knowledge ought to reach the common people if the governments did not want to benefit from it.

Their opinion worked wonders and President Roosevelt called a meeting of army officers and scientists and discussed the expansion of the Manhattan Project. As a result, Einstein's association with the project became firm.

The project was placed under the supervision of America's National Security Research Committee and a special committee was formed regarding science matters. The work of this Committee was to inform the government about the latest development in the research on nuclear fission. The committee dealt with America's national security.

Now Einstein demanded from the government that elaborate experiments be carried out and practical use of the research be found. It meant that it was necessary to keep the process of nuclear fission continuous and use it in a practical way. He demanded more finance for the Manhattan Project.

The Roosevelt administration made Oppenheimer head of the project. At the same time, the whole world came to know the practical use of nuclear fission. The demands to develop nuclear weapon rose in Britain. Work regarding this had also started in France and research was gaining pace in Germany.

People had started to visualise the future nuclear bomb in their minds. They thought that the bomb would not be heavy. Every country was in the race to manufacture the nuclear bomb in order to gain supremacy over other countries. In April, 1940, Einstein informed the Roosevelt administration that the first stage of this project was completed. He also said that the second stage would be quite difficult.

On December 6, 1941, Japan attacked Pearl Harbor. The Americans suffered a great loss by this sudden attack. Thus America entered the war. This incidence increased the pace of the Nuclear Bomb Project. The work on extracting

Uranium-235 became faster. It had faced many obstacles. A gas diffusion technique was being used.

Einstein's friends were also surprised by his changed attitude. His work had been limited to theoretical physics only. Now, he participated in practical experiments also. In the beginning, peace-loving Einstein encouraged scientists to abstain from work related to war. Now, he himself was contributing a lot to the development of a destructive weapon. He was doing it happily as he believed it to be vital for the country which gave him shelter. His equation of E = mc2 was the main base of this bomb.

He talked often in a philosophical way. He used to say that man was created by God. If God had not created him, how could he gain the rights provided by God? If the facts had not been so, he would have only got the rights mentioned in the constitution. Constitutions did not exist at the time of our forefathers but they managed to fight untruth. He believed that the war being fought by America was a fight against untruth.

With the passage of time, Einstein gained importance in America. He also got a luxurious office. His step son-in-law Dmitri Marianoff, who had divorced his step daughter, Margot, began to write his biography.

But Einstein was not affected by it. The writer claimed that he had been living with Einstein's family for the last eight years, but Einstein denied it. He said that he had lived with them for just a few months.

The book was published and became quite popular. What was written was not harmful, but Einstein refused to approve it.

He wanted his name to be used only for important works. Once a message from President Roosevelt was required for the help of institutes in Palestine. Roosevelt had refused. When Einstein asked him, he agreed.

At that time, several scientific meetings were organised. There was a great demand for Einstein. The four hundredth death anniversary of Copernicus was celebrated. Copernicus was considered to be a revolutionary scientist. Einstein, the current revolutionary scientist, was invited to Carnegie Hall. Along with Einstein, T.H. Morgon, who had created the design of the helicopter, and Henry Ford were also invited. On the occasion, in his short speech, Einstein declared Copernicus his Guru.

Einstein had to face many peculiarities in America during the war. Whenever he wrote letters to his relatives in Europe and to his friends in Germany, the Americans would open and investigate them. When the letter reached the destined country, it was also opened there and investigated. Many scientists, whose research work got disturbed due to the war, came to Einstein for help. Wilhelm Reich had been working on biological energy for a long time. He had also worked as Faraday's assistant from 1922 to 1930 in Vienna. He was not a good physicist but he was a good psychologist. When his work was affected by the war, he wrote to Einstein in December 1940. Einstein invited him to his house on January 13, 1941 and talked to him for five hours. Later, a controversy arose over an issue.

During the war, he accepted all types of work against the Nazis. To collect finance in 1943, he was told to donate his original research papers of 1905. Unluckily, these papers had got destroyed during his migration. But Einstein prepared them again and donated them all. His original manuscripts were priced in lakhs of dollars at that time. Several of them are still preserved in the Library of Congress.

Einstein also did some work for the American Navy for a short duration. Because of his capabilities, he was made a member of many committees. Thanks to his suggestions, there were many ongoing projects related to defence at Princeton. He was associated with the defence department in some places, as a scientist, and in other places, as an industrial scholar. For two years, he had associated with the Department as an advisor whose job was to carry out research work on explosives.

During the war, services of almost all the scientists were used. While the bomb was being made, the technique of dropping it was being developed. Scientists like Dr. Von Newman, Dr. John Kirkwood, Dr. George Gamow were involved in the technique.

Due to his growing age and declining health, Einstein was relieved from going to Washington for the research work. George was given the responsibility. He was instructed to contact Einstein at Princeton for requirement and fulfill whatever was needed for the work. Every Friday, George visited Princeton by train. Along with him, in his briefcase, he used to carry the secret documents of the Naval Project. George would discuss the tunnels that were built under water, bombs that were to be dropped by the planes on aircraft carriers and similar proposals and techniques. When George received Einstein's approval, he returned to the Admiralty. It increased his confidence. Many apprehensions that Einstein had would prove true in practical experiments.

During the period, he was in a dilemma. Perhaps, that was the reason for not giving him full information about the Manhattan Project. Scientists like Szilard, Fermi, Compton, Vigner, etc. were totally associated with the Manhattan Project. But Einstein could guess the progress of work because the progress of the uranium industry was clearly visible.

Niels Bohr, somehow, reached Sweden in a small boat and came to America. He met Einstein at Princeton. He was travelling on a British passport in the name of John Baker.

It seemed to Einstein that for the downfall of Hitler, these nuclear weapons were a necessity. In future, they could be widely misused. He used to discuss this fact with the people he met. He also mentioned it in the letter he wrote to Niels Bohr.

His apprehensions were true. Every large country of the world was in the race for nuclear weapons. Soviet Russia through its scientists sent a proposal to Niels Bohr that he could come with his family and stay in the Soviet Union and do his research there. He was tempted very much.

At that time, he was in England. The news reached Churchill. Investigation started. Bohr was finding it difficult to answer. Later, Roosevelt invited Bohr and heard his story with sympathy. He understood that Bohr was being harassed unnecessarily. It could not be imagined that he would provide secret information about the nuclear bomb project to the Russians. Many scientists took Bohr's side.

The development of the nuclear bomb continued. They were deciding where to drop the bomb after it had been developed. The Germans were talking of driving away Jewish physicists. The research work there was badly affected. The shortage of theoretical physics, which was mocked at as Jewish physics, had become a sore. Now, they started to feel the need for the same Theory of Relativity which had once been bitterly opposed. Germany started to lag behind in the development of the nuclear bomb. One reason for this was that in the early years of World War II, Germany had gained victories and did not feel the need for a nuclear bomb. They were quite late in assessing their mistakes.

Ironically, the project of the nuclear bomb in Germany was carried out in the village where Elsa was born. Scientists like Heisenberg and Hahn were doing their work along with a dozen of scientists. The project was named 'Alsos'.

The American Secret Service had achieved success in acquiring information about this project by the end of 1944. To end the war quickly, America itself had prepared to drop the bomb on Japan. The scientists, who had been working for years on the project of development of the nuclear bomb, had started to blame themselves for the upcoming devastation. They wanted it to be used just to create fear.

The period was full of upheavals. The Alliance Nations had bombarded Germany's residential areas heavily. Einstein approved of their action. He said that an organised power could be encountered only by another organised power. He even said that if the opponent was keen to destroy you, you needed to be powerful.

Eventually, the major devastation occurred at Hiroshima and Nagasaki. Japan surrendered. World War II came to an end. Einstein was sixty-six years old and took retirement from Princeton Institute. His equation E = mc2 had proved itself through devastating results. Many people were eager to know his reactions. He said that nuclear energy was a natural energy just like the energy in the body by which one can row a boat. He also said that, in future, this energy would be used commercially in a big way.

□

After the Destruction

The Second World War had ended, but the ruins of destruction were everywhere. Discussions were held on the treatment to be meted out to Germany and Japan who had lost the war. In Palestine, it was becoming difficult to avert conflicts between the Jews and the Arabs. Russia, America and Britain had been united during the war. After the war, every country was finding it difficult to accept Russia.

Einstein was living in his residence on Mercer Street. He was considering himself responsible for the death of one lakh twenty thousand innocent people. In August 1945, Albert Einstein expressed his views on nuclear war through the American Broadcasting Company. He said that the formula of developing the destructive nuclear bomb should be only with an international governing body. This probable administrator of the world should directly interfere with those countries, where the majorities were carrying out atrocities on the minorities.

He made America and Britain realise their responsibilities because both had the formula to create the nuclear bomb. It seemed to him that soon this formula would reach Soviet Russia also. There was turmoil in Spain and Argentina but Einstein believed that those problems could be solved without any war.

Einstein was upset with Soviet Russia because of its undemocratic conditions. The people of Soviet Russia did not enjoy full freedom in education and scientific work. Several Russian scientists were taking asylum in western countries. Due to this, tensions between the nations intensified.

Despite this, Einstein hoped that the international government of his dreams would become a reality. In November, 1947, Einstein, wrote an open letter to the highest council of the United Nations. He suggested that the governments of all countries should surrender their rights on their own to an international governing body.

People considered his thoughts idealistic. They thought that such arrangements could not be made overnight. Einstein repeatedly said that an immediate step was necessary. Though the nuclear bomb had caused massive destruction and people were quite aware of it yet they were eager to know about other uses of nuclear energy. Efforts were being made to collect more and more information and make it available to the common people. A committee was formed of about fifty educational, religious and city organisations. Einstein was also a member. To make the committee effective, efforts were made to raise funds for it.

The scientists who were associated with nuclear power were also getting united. Einstein was made president of their committee. A countrywide movement started in America to create new awareness among the people and to ensure survival of the human race in the nuclear age. Einstein believed that powerful and destructive weapons existed in this world, and unless the people gave up their narrow thoughts of nationalism, there would be total destruction. It was also necessary to start the disarmament process quickly; otherwise, freedom would become extinct in the whole world.

America was proceeding towards the development of a hydrogen bomb. Einstein opposed it. He observed that no country could be prevented from moving in that direction unless and until the whole world was ready for disarmament.

Einstein was not getting much importance in the period of chaos after the war. His friends were trying to force him to come to Palestine. They wanted Einstein to live in Palestine and carry forward his scientific work. Weizmann invited him to visit Palestine for four to six weeks. But Einstein refused this invitation because of his deteriorating health. While his view of an international government was considered impractical, all relating information to nuclear energy was handed over to the army.

Einstein started repenting. Though photographers were still eager to take his picture and the common people still listened to him with respect, yet he felt defeated. He said several times, "We are physicists, not politicians; to get into politics is not our cup of tea."

But he continued his efforts to organise scholars. Around two hundred educators, religious leaders and writers gathered in Princeton on the occasion of his seventy-fifth birthday. Though he himself was not able to attend this meeting, yet he was deeply involved in it.

Germany had become stagnant after the war. In October 1946, Einstein was invited to become a member of the Bavaria Academy. He remembered the killings of the Jews by the Nazis but expressed his happiness over the invitation. Otto Hahn suggested that he should become a foreign member of his organisation, but Einstein humbly declined. He said that the mentality of the German scholars was no different from the mentality of the masses.

His hometown of Ulm requested him to accept honorary citizenship, but he didn't. When people questioned him, he said that the memories of the massacres were still fresh in his mind. In this condition, it was difficult to be associated with any German organisation.

In September 1950, he wrote to his old friend, Born, that though every person at birth had the same nature, the Germans have more dangerous tendencies. He also wrote, "We have probably learnt something from these painful experiences."

After two years, Born took retirement from Edinburg and returned to Germany. He believed that the Americans were more ruthless killers as proved by Hiroshima and Nagasaki incidents. It was difficult to decide what was more brutal—forcing the Jews into gas chambers or dropping the bomb on Hiroshima.

During his last days, Einstein was not able to get rid of his dilemma. The newspapers of that period were blaming Hitler for all the destruction, but Einstein believed that he was not the only one responsible. He heard of Max Planck's death. A great scientist, Planck's life was also full of sorrows. His first son had died. His second son was convicted for attempting to kill Hitler and was hanged in 1944. Einstein and Planck had a close association between 1913 and 1947. After Planck's death, Einstein, in his letter to Madam Planck, wrote about his good old times with him.

Einstein was dissatisfied with America. In his letter written to Plesch in 1947, Einstein said that America had changed since 1928. It had become aggressive and dangerous. By 'highlighting the terror of Russian communism, it was justifying its own cruel deeds'.

There was a time when he was tired of Germany's activities and planned to get out of Germany. Now, he was receiving offers of grants from all over the world. Many of his relatives had settled in South America and they were inviting him. In 1948, he was invited to Israel, but he said that he had become too old. One of his friends said that he was only of sixty-nine years. According to Jewish traditions, he had to live fifty-one years more to reach the age of Moses. □

The Birth of Israel

The nations of the world were looking forward to a new era after the war. The process of forming a separate nation for the Jews was in an advanced stage. Einstein dreamt about a Jewish nation that would always maintain friendly relations with neighbouring Arab countries. Thus, it did not require an armed force. He was strictly against extreme nationalism.

At that time, the clamour for freedom had started in colonies all over the world. Small countries which were under British rule were slowly gaining freedom. In Palestine also, changes were in the offing, but there was also growing tension.

Einstein's love and devotion for his Jewish brethren was increasing. When he was asked to help collect funds for the new nation, his response was instant. He wrote an article which was auctioned. It fetched 5,000 dollars.

At last in May 1948, Israel was created. Weizmann became its first president, but he soon died. Einstein was in his seventies by then. He was physically very weak, but people still had a lot of faith in him.

In 1952, he was requested to hold the post of President of Israel. The post was more of an honour and it had nothing to do with politics. This was a gesture from his grateful race for his contribution to build a Jewish nation.

This news hit the headlines in newspapers in Tel Aviv. Israeli Minister, David Ben Gurion, proudly remarked that there was no Jew in the world greater than Einstein. If he accepted this offer, his selection would be just a formality. Einstein did not, however, consider the offer seriously. When the New York Times asked for his reaction, he declined to make any statement.

Soon, Israel's ambassador to America, Abba Eban, contacted him. Now Einstein did not have any option but to refuse quite sternly. During the period, his residence at Mercer Street used to be haunted by journalists.

Eban had come at the formal request of the Israeli Prime Minister. He requested him repeatedly to accept the post but Einstein stuck to his decision.

On November 18, 1952, he received a letter from Israeli minister, David Ben Gurien, saying that he should accept the post and move to Israel. The government would make all arrangements for his scientific work.

Einstein became quite emotional. He said, "I am thankful to you for this offer but I am very sorry that I will not be able to accept it." Narrating his reason, he said, "I don't possess the required qualities and experience to fulfill government responsibilities. Though I am quite attached to my Jewish brothers, yet it is beyond my capacity to fulfill these responsibilities."

Einstein's rejection of the offer was variously interpreted by different people. Some people said that it was difficult for a scientist to become the president of a nation. Others opined that Weizmann, who was a biochemist, could become the President, Einstein, too, could become the President.

Perhaps, Einstein did not want to restrict himself to a single country.

He always remained sensitive regarding Israel. He was apprehensive about the aggressive behaviour of the neighbouring Arab nations. He was also worried that Russia and Czechoslovakia were not only creating hatred in the Arab nations, but they were also selling large amounts of dangerous weapons to Egypt.

Though America was making fighter jets and other weapons available to Israel, Einstein was not satisfied. It seemed to him that America could try to appease the Arab nations. Through this process, it could sacrifice the welfare of Israel.

Israel was established in May 1948. In April 1955, the Israeli Embassy asked him to give a speech on its Foundation Day.

The manuscript of his speech was prepared. The Israeli ambassador, Abba Eban, and his assistant arrived in Israel with the manuscript. Nobody expected that Einstein would not be there to hear the reaction to his speech.

□

Epilogue

Despite all the dilemma, Einstein decided to spend his last days in America. In his letter to his relative Lina, who was living in Latin America, he wrote that seventeen expensive years had been spent in America and, probably, the rest of his life would be spent there. Princeton was now his home.

Doctors had imposed several restrictions on Einstein. There was total restriction on tobacco. Despite the fact, he kept a small pipe with him and kept the tobacco hidden. He used to ask others for a matchbox to light it.

One of his old friends, who was a doctor, had fled from Berlin and reached New York. He had given him strict instructions that he should only have fat-free, salt-free food. Once after dinner, he was offered chocolates. They were very tempting. He exclaimed, "The devil has imposed restrictions on all things we like. Either our health deteriorates or the mind becomes polluted." His friend, who was eating with him, questioned, "Why devil, why not God?" Einstein immediately answered that it did not make a difference.

Both have similar qualities. One has positive qualities and the other had negative qualities.

Once a doctor came to him with medicine. He asked Einstein how he would prefer the medicine—as a liquid or a solid. Einstein accepted the medicine in the form of drops. He keenly observed the drops of medicine falling into the glass full of water. He quickly drank it. After this, he asked doctor, "Are you feeling better?"

He was severely ill in 1917. By 1945, his physical condition had become quite bad. He had his first operation in 1945 and second operation in 1948. Some complexities had developed in his main artery and it appeared that he had very little time left.

Owing to his weak health, he hardly moved out of Princeton. Most of his time was spent in his room or in his bed. A bulb hanging over his head used to remain lit. With paper and pencil in his hand, he used to think and keep on writing. He wanted to get rid of the situation of indeterminacy in physics.

He wanted to consult his old friends regularly. He got to know Max Born in 1916. They differed on many subjects. During World War II, Einstein had contributed to the development of the nuclear bomb for America, but Born refused to do the same work for Britain. They had different opinions regarding Germans also. Einstein invited Born to stay in Princeton, but in vain.

Niels Bohr visited Princeton regularly. He was involved in Princeton Institute. He made a great contribution to the book Albert Einstein: Philosophical Scientist prepared for Einstein's seventieth birthday. He also had long discussions with him. As a result, serious conflicts arose.

Different people knew Einstein in different ways. Einstein was aware of the mocking statements made about him. Once he wrote in a letter to one of his Jewish friends, "People know me as a person who doesn't wear socks."

In his last days, he was involved in combining the theory of relativity, theory of gravity and developing unified theory. His daily activities used to be very simple. He would have breakfast between nine and ten, when he read all the political news published in the daily newspapers. In winter around half past ten in the morning, the institute car would pick him up. He walked back in the afternoon. In summer, he would walk to the institute and return by car due to the heat.

Sometimes, his assistant would be with him. Sometimes, he used to give a lift to strangers. On the way, he cracked jokes and laughed and made others laugh.

He worked at the institute till one o'clock. He got involved with several mathematical equations. At one o'clock sharp, he would pack his papers in his old briefcase and go home. He was asked to keep a permanent assistant for himself, but he refused. He wanted people to do their own work.

After lunch at half one past, he rested for a while. Post afternoon he had tea and met visitors. He read the letters which came daily by post. He ate dinner at half past six. Afterwards, he did some work and wrote letters.

Sometimes, he turned on the radio. In his leisure time, he listened to violin played by Bach or Mozart. On Sundays, his friends would take him to the countryside or the seashore which was almost an hour away by car. Now he did not like to meet people.

When IBM invited him to inaugurate their computer, he did not even reply. They were worried because this was a big event. Later, it was revealed that Einstein had thrown the invitation into the dustbin.

His room was decorated with strange things. It had religious pictures and items, a statue of a Chinese philosopher who looked like a beggar and Italian Christian paintings.

After Elsa's death, Helen Dukas had taken over the running of his house. She used to buy things for him and looked after his house. She filed his letters and complained about the inadequate space for the letters. But she took good care of Einstein.

Einstein's step-daughter, Margot, and his younger sister, Maja also lived with him during his last days. Einstein was quite fond of his sister. He liked Maja's way of speaking and her childish behaviour. A lot of her habits were like those of her elder brother. Maja had suffered from joint pain since 1946 and was unable to move. After 1950, Maja's condition deteriorated and most of Margot's time was taken in looking after her. Till the end, Maja was interested in her studies. Einstein also had to bear the loss of his sister in his last days. Maja died in December 1951.

Till the last moment, Einstein did meditation. He thought deeply about Gandhiji's principles and continued to think about how to make them a reality all over the world.

He enjoyed himself anidst the beauties of nature. He was against spending whole life in work. It seemed to him that this would cause abnormalities in a person. He was influenced by Eddington's book based on beauty. He considered four people to be the greatest in this world. These people were Newton, Maxwell, Mahatma Gandhi and a German musician. In his last days, he was influenced by Dr. Albert Schweitzer.

He also continued thinking about religious matters till his last days. He used to say that he was not ready to worship any God out of fear. He could not have blind faith. He could not even prove the existence of an absolute God.

He believed that brotherhood should prevail all over the world. Everyone was different; this should be taken into account. "We know many things, understand them but it is impossible to prove everything. Our minds can think only up to a level."

Einstein's mind worked at the speed of light in his last days. He thought about every good and evil incident in his life. He also thought about his first marriage.

In the beginning of 1955, the atmosphere in Germany had totally changed. The Germans recalled Einstein's research papers, the great work he had done in the scientific world and its upcoming fiftieth anniversary. Plans were made to organise a conference in Berne and Berlin on this occasion. Einstein was requested to attend the conference. Einstein refused the invitation because of his physical weakness. A conference was organised in Switzerland also, but Einstein was not able to attend it.

In the middle of February, 1955, Einstein got a letter from Bertrand Russell. Both had strongly opposed World War I but believed that World War II could not be averted. Both were against extremism and thought that the development of the hydrogen bomb was unnecessary and devastating. But they had their differences. Despite conflicting thoughts and unfavourable conditions, Einstein continued to work in the Kaiser Wilhelm Institute. Russell did not hesitate to go to jail. Einstein continued to be mentally upset but Russell continued to protest at public places. Einstein did not believe in violent protests, but Russell did. He frequently expressed his anger.

On February 11, 1955, Russell wrote a firm letter to Einstein and asked him to protest against the mad race in nuclear weapons. He said that the race would lead to destruction of humanity. Scientists like him should openly protest. At least, six scientists under his leadership should release a declaration letter and it would be much better if these people belonged to different schools of thought. The appeal should be made to the neutral countries to destroy the probability of a third world war.

On February 16, Einstein replied that the declaration should contain the signatures of twelve of the best scientists and include scientists even from communist countries. Niels Bohr would lead the neutral countries.

At last, on April 5, the letter was ready. It expressed concern about a probable war. Special stress was given to the destructive power of the hydrogen bomb. All nations were requested to sort out their disputes in a peaceful way so that the world might not end up in another world war.

In his final days, Einstein was so concerned about peace that he wrote a letter to Pandit Nehru and appealed to him to work for world peace. He was quite apprehensive about the Chinese government's intentions.

How much Einstein honoured Russell is evident from the fact that he told Russell, "You are the commander of this peace movement, but I am just a small soldier in it. You give orders; I will follow."

Einstein realised that he had a very little time left. He knew that he was nearing death. He took care of himself and covered himself with blankets even when the weather was not cold. He wanted to live a long life in order to oppose the Cold War and check the growing threat of war against Israel.

The names of the scientists, whose signatures would be in the declaration of April 11, were confirmed. It was also decided that there would be a very big conference at which selected scientists from more than a dozen countries including Russia, Britain and America would participate. The very next day, Einstein's health deteriorated. Despite the fact, he did not send for a doctor. Helen realised the seriousness of the situation and she rang up Margot who was in a local hospital because of her own illness.

Though he suffered from severe pain yet he kept himself involved in the publicity and in campaigning for celebrating the Independence Day of Israel. By then, five articles had been prepared wherein there was a mention of probable conflicts between Israel and Egypt.

He also mentioned the conflicts between the democratic world (independent world) and the communist world. He thought it relevant to call it a conflict between the East and the West instead of mentioning Socialist and Democrat. Though he believed that the world was round yet the words 'east' and 'west' were antonyms.

His situation became worse on April 13. He met the Ambassador of Israel and Janos Plesch in the morning. After discussions, he added some more points to his memorandum. By noon, the visitors had departed. Einstein became very tired. Though he was not hungry yet he had some light food and rested in his bed but he became unconscious very soon. Helen sent for the doctor. The doctor arrived soon with his two assistants. He did an ECG and injected morphine. After the injection, Einstein slept calmly.

On April 14, a group of doctors from New York arrived. But they were in a dilemma whether to do surgery or not. At that time, there were little chances of life after complicated operations.

Einstein was aware of his situation. He very often said "Let this sore get burnt by itself." He never agreed to undergo an operation. He used to ask the doctors when he would die after the sore had burst. The doctor replied that it could be a sudden death; it could come after an hour or after months.

The pain increased. The doctor advised that he should be taken to the hospital. Einstein refused. Usually, doctors do not give importance to the wishes of patients. Keeping in view the personality of Einstein, they were hesitant. They said that Helen would not be able to take care of the situation. They advocated that Einstein should go to the hospital as his position was quite critical. On his way to the hospital, he kept talking to everyone. After he had been shifted to the hospital bed from the trolley, he asked for his spectacles and writing material. He felt that his last moments should not be wasted. He also telephoned his relatives at home.

Margot came on a wheelchair to meet him. Einstein's appearance was so changed that it was difficult for his daughter to recognise him. But Einstein's humorous nature was still evident. He even mocked his doctors.

Einstein did not like the use of his name unnecessarily. He expressed some of his desires and said that his house should not be transformed into a museum. He also requested the Princeton Institute to make his office available for the use of scientists. He knew that his house and his office would become a holy place for scientists. He also said that the gifts given to him—the momentos, the letters—should be sent to India if desired by someone.

Einstein was sure that his possessions and letters would be sold for many dollars. Now, he wanted to be free of this give-and-take business. He believed that his brain was exceptional. So, he desired that after his death they should study his head. The last rites of his body should be done and the remains should be thrown into an unknown place.

His son Hans Albert Einstein and the literary executive Otto Nathan arrived just before his death. Einstein talked about science. Afterwards, he talked about politics. He also expressed his view on the threat that might arise due to the ban on weapons in Germany.

It was Sunday afternoon. The doctors hoped for progress in Einstein's condition. In the evening, he experienced pain. The doctors gave him an injection so that he might sleep.

Dr. Dean was the last to attend to him at 11 p.m. After some hours, it seemed to the nurse that he was having difficulty in breathing. She was terrified and called another nurse for help and took whatever steps she could.

At the last moment, he murmured in German. He had travelled to many countries across the world and was well acquainted with several languages. His place of origin was Germany and the first language he learnt was German.

His relations with Germany were strange. While living there, he became a world-famous luminary. He believed, "Naturally, humans beings are violent, but the Germans are more violent."

Perhaps, in his last moments, he repented not being able to visit Germany and for encouraging President Roosevelt to build a nuclear bomb.

It was not clear whether he was repenting or he wanted to say something. His nurse was not able to understand what he was murmuring in German. He took a deep breath and left this world on April 18, 1955.

□

After the Departure

Einstein's first wife, Mileva, his second wife, Elsa, and his younger sister, Maja had already left this world before Einstein. His second son, Edward, suffered from a mental disorder. In 1933 he was admitted to a mental asylum. In 1965, he died.

Einstein's first son's life was comparatively better. He got a chance to work as a professor in California University. He worked in the field of hydraulics.

After Einstein's death his brain was preserved. Scientists regularly investigated it, but it seemed to them that his brain was no different from that of any other normal human being.

In 1996, scientists came to the conclusion that the size of his brain was bigger than normal. But it was still a mystery how Albert Einstein used this minor difference to reveal the secrets of the world.

His theory of relativity and theory of magnetism remained a puzzle. As scientists were performing practical experiments on his theories, they were gaining prestige. As time passed, a better and more effective accelerator developed. With its help, particles were made so powerful that their speed became equal to the speed of light.

A space mission based on Einstein's theory was organised. Several rockets and satellites were launched. In 1969, when the American astronauts reached the moon in the rocket named Apollo, the difference between calculations based on Einstein's theory and reality seemed to be minimal, hardly 20 inches. Thus, it was proved that the general theory of relativity was so close to reality.

Einstein was opposed even after his death. Between 1960 and 1970, a scientist by named Herbert Dingle tried to prove the theory of relativity to be untenable but he was not successful. In a similar way, when collections of his articles were published, opposition was generated, but did not garner any support.

Albert Einstein hoped to combine all the theories and make an integrated one, i.e. Grand Unified theory. But this dream is still not fulfilled.

Scientists began to unite over the string theory. According to this theory, the particle is not the basic matter but strings are the basic matter which just have length and are devoid of thickness. Two strings can combine to make a single string.

Einstein had started working on it long before and he had spent most of his life in search of the fourth dimension. Till date, eleven dimensions have been discovered under the theory. This theory is still not mature and investigations are going on.

In 1979, Einstein's birth centenary was celebrated. All over the world, conferences and seminars were organised to honour him. Long discussions were held everywhere, i.e. Bonn, Jerusalem, West Germany, Princeton, New York, and the Smithsonian Institute. The central point of discussion was the composition of the universe. A big exhibition was organised on the occasion in Washington.

Even after his death, Einstein remained a topic of discussion not only amongst the scientists but also among all peace makers.

His not forgiving Germany was not wholly approved of by the world. People were astonished that Einstein who was born in Germany had so much hatred for it. Since 1920 Einstein hoped that Israel and the Arabs would maintain cordial relations, but it was not possible. After his death the Arab countries and Israel had severe conflicts and several wars were fought between the two rivals.

Einstein's dream of a world government is yet to be fulfilled. The world continues with the race for nuclear and other weapons. The discussions on disarmament continues but without any notable results.

By the large Einstein is still remembered as a great scientist as well as a preacher of peace.

In 1999, Time magazine recognised, Einstein as an 'Important personality of the 20th century. Year 2005 was celebrated as centenary year of his famous, wonderful research papers which changed the various theories prevailing at that time.

□

Theory of Light

Since ancient time, man has been experiencing light and thinking about its nature.

Everything that existed in the universe had been broadly divided into two categories. One was called matter which was physical and the other was called energy which was only experienced like heat, sound, light, etc.

Since the Aristotelian era, a number of theories had been propounded about light. Earlier, it was accepted that light is basically a collection of tiny particles which gets reflected when collide with other material. Probably, this theory is based on the fact that when light comes through a hole in the roof to the ground, we find a number of tiny particles. The law of reflection can be explained with this hypothesis. Other incidences can't be explained, as refraction of light is also seen. Apart from this, light comes from the sun and it is difficult to believe that these particles can travel such a long journey on their own.

In due course, it was believed that light acts as a wave. People started believing that as sound waves move further in the air, the light also moves. But the movement of sound in vacuum is not possible as there is no medium. But the light from the sun reaches the earth though there is a vacuum in between.

People, who believed that light moves in as a wave, started imagining that there must be a medium though it is not visible or can't be experienced. This invisible medium was given a name: Ether.

The following were the properties of Ether, the hypothetical medium:

1. It is invisible.
2. It has no weight.
3. The sound waves can't move through it.
4. It can't be inhaled during respiration. Similarly, neither can it be smelt or tasted.
5. This can't become an obstacle to astronomical bodies like stars, planets, etc.

This hypothetical medium 'ether' also couldn't help explain all the properties of light. It was observed, "When light falls on some objects like tin, electrons are ejected." By the end of the nineteenth century, J.J. Thomson had already identified the electrons. It was believed that the elements like tin have electrons loosely held and the moment they gain energy, they become active and start moving freely.

Apart from the above confusion, there was another complexity. The above activity, which was named Photo Electric Theory, also has a variety. Some elements like Titanium and Uranium do not release electrons when red light falls on them but the moment blue light falls on them, the release process of electrons starts. This simply means that there is a distinct difference between blue light and red light.

It was also found that the waves creating blue light are shorter. This means shorter waves are having more energy. They have more capacity to eject electrons from the material on which they fall.

It can be compared with the situation of a man boating in a lake. If he rows faster, he will displace more water and if he rows slower, he will displace less water.

But the above comparison also couldn't explain the phenomenon fully. It was seen that even after throwing red light for longer duration the emission of electrons could not start.

In the Einstein era, a number of scientists were struggling at various fronts. Max Planck, who was a close friend of Einstein, was investigating black body. He was confronted with a question, 'Which colour is emitted from black body? Is it black radiation?'

But it was found that the colour of the black body depends on its temperature. When it is cold, it looks black. When it is hot, it emits red radiation. The rest of the colours emitted are not so much prominent. As the temperature of the body rises, the changes in colour are seen. Colours like orange, yellow increase. A situation comes when other colours are also in sufficient proportion and the body looks like white.

Einstein kept on looking at the universe and found that there are a number of stars including the sun in the sky. In fact, these are also black bodies. He prepared an equation between their colours and temperatures. Thus, a method was evolved to know the approximate temperature of a particular star.

During the period, a thought emerged in the mind of Max Planck. He concluded, "If light is a radiation and it behaves like a wave, it should have a definite velocity. Every vibration moves further with a definite velocity."

Simultaneously, Einstein put forward a theory and informed the world that light in fact moves forward as a bunch which was named 'photon'. These 'photons' have a definite quantum of light.

At the same time, he also told that the wavelength of the light we measure is actually the wavelength of the photons. With the help of this wavelength, the energy contained in this can also be measured. The vibration of red light is slower. Accordingly, the energy contained in this is less. On the other hand, the blue light is having photons that vibrate faster.

Einstein explained more about these photons and said that these are, in fact, like small stars or points and they collide with our eyes in hundreds of numbers every second.

With this theory, it was now easier to explain the photo electric effect clearly. Red light is not able to eject electrons from some of the material as it does not have sufficient energy.

Einstein had a capacity to explain the phenomena with unique examples. He explained, "If somebody has entered a pit to take out a ball lying below and he uses less or insufficient energy, he will not be able to take out the ball. The ball will come out only when high/sufficient energy is used."

With this new theory, all theories based on hypothetical 'Ether' disappeared. It was concluded that light is not a wave and it does not require medium for movement.

But the matter didn't end here. Other scientists kept on experimenting on the theory evolved by Einstein. The scientist named De Broglie found that the electrons and other micro-sized particles, which have definite shapes and sizes, also behave like waves in many ways.

At that time, several scientists were engaged in understanding the unusual behaviour of the matter. Niels Bohr explained these behaviours by taking help of the theory of Einstein. For example, we find that the light emitted by sodium vapour lamp is of orange colour. When we see the items of orange colour, there are various shades available. Out of them some are having yellowish shade and some reddish shade. Many of them have a mixture of shades. When hot sodium vapour emits radiation, only two shades are emitted and both are similar. Similar behaviour is shown by other hot gases also and the colours emerged also look similar.

Niels Bohr further explained this process and said that when a material is heated, extra energy is inserted inside it in this process. A part of this energy is taken by the electrons. As this energy is increased, the electrons drift away from its nucleus. But they do not go out of the boundary of the atom and remain at a certain distance from the nucleus of the atom.

After some time, these electrons start coming back to their place. In this process, they emit their energy. Initially, Niels Bohr was not satisfied with the Photon theory and was considering the light as a continuous wave. However, later he agreed that every electron emits definite amount of energy. Since all sodium atoms are alike and move from one position to other in a similar condition, hence they emit similar kind of energy. That is why the photons emitted depend upon the energy. They have similar colour. That is why a hot sodium lamp emits similar light.

As a follow-up to this process, Einstein further disclosed that if a group of atoms is alike and their energy level is at definite higher level, if one electron occupies its original position, the others will also keep on occupying their original positions. Thus, their photons will generate a very powerful beam of light having only one colour.

As a result, Einstein dreamt about laser. However, it could materialise only in 1960 for the first time.

During that era, all the scientists were involved in solving these mysteries. Finally, all of them came to the same platform and started accepting that light, electron and other types of particles in some ways behave as particles and in some other ways behave as waves. Thus they have dual characters.

But these mysteries were not fully solved. One ambiguity was that when electron is excited, it is difficult to pinpoint exactly when it will release photons.

At that time, it was believed that every incidence has a definite cause.

Afterwards, Albert started imagining about the structure of the universe. He agreed that this universe is fabricated by very small tiny particles and tiny energy sources (Photon). It is a matter of incidence that ancient Indian scholars have also thrown light on the contribution of matter and energy in the structure of the universe. Sir Issac Newton also imagined a similar pattern a few centuries ago.

However, Einstein started demonstrating the relations of matter and energy by way of pure mathematical equations. He had already proved that matter and energy, i.e. electrons and photons, behave similarly in various cases.

But the Quantum Theory developed during that era had indicated that it was difficult to predict about the amount of energy in an object. Also it was not possible to predict its exact speed. This indeterminacy is negligible in bigger objects but this is quite important in case of smaller objects like electrons and photons.

For example, if we wish to predict the exact amount of energy and exact speed of an electron in the duration of one nanosecond, it is rather impossible. At present, instead of measuring the speed, the measuring instruments available disturb the position and speed of the particle.

During the era of Einstein, more and more information was being generated about radioactivity. It was known that some atoms are unstable. Thus, the faith on indeterminacy was on the increase.

During the development of Quantum Theory, various types of arguments emerged. For example, if a coin is tossed in the air or on the table, it will have one position when it falls down, *i.e.* either heads or tails.

As long as the coin is in the air or tossing on the table, the position of the coin is uncertain. During this position, it is difficult to prove the existence of the coin. In order to prove its existence, the coin is to be held by applying force. Thus it can be said that the existence of an item can't be proved unless it is measured. However, during this process, the situation of the object changes as the moving coin comes to standstill.

Similarly, the various particles also move. However, after measuring them, it can be known in which direction they are moving. When energy is used by a measuring instrument to know the direction of the spin of an electron, it may happen that energy used changes the direction of that electron.

Hence, the scientists can only speculate. Let us take an instance. While watching T.V. a viewer speculates what will happen in the next scene. Though quantum theory was vague, yet it was possible to explain various incidents with its help.

Apart from this, it was proving practical also. With its help, the explanation of light and other situations / incidents will be like this:

1. In some cases, the light and particles behave as waves.
2. In some cases, the light and particles behave as particles.
3. There is a limit to know about a particle.
4. This universe is fuzzy which means that the particles in it are moving neither with a definite speed nor their position is definitely known.
5. Many times, it is not clearly known why a particular incident is occurring in a certain way.
6. Unless the position and speed of the particles are measured, it is not clear what they are doing.

However, Albert was definitely clear that there were some deep mysteries which would be solved later. He determined that he would continue research in this direction and also take help of other scientists like Niels Bohr. He would do all possible efforts to solve these mysteries.

He tried to develop another concept about particles. Later on, people started believing that these particles are in the form of pairs. One spins in a clockwise direction and the other in an anti-clockwise direction. Both can't spin in the same direction. If one is measured, the other is also affected.

Scientists kept on investigating the above theory even after the demise of Einstein.

□

Nothing Absolute

Since ancient time, the scientists, the astronomers and the philosophers had been thinking in depth about various phenomena of the universe. They always tried to find out how and why these incidents occur. In India, Aryabhatta, Bhaskaracharya and many others had formulated a number of equations and explained many of the phenomena which are considered a truth even today. In the same line, the western scientists like Sir Issac Newton, etc. explained about phenomena of the rotations of planets, stars, etc.

They also explained that these astronomical bodies are large objects constructed by tiny particles and these are hard objects. They have got a definite mass. The forces of attraction and repulsion act on them on the basis of their masses. Due to constant attraction and repulsion in the universe: there is movement as well as balance.

If we see carefully the movements of these planets, stars, etc. then we may feel that a game of snooker is going on at a large scale. It is full of excitement.

Newton not only defined the laws of motion but also explained that if one object is pushed, how it will move. He also gave clear mathematical equations which were used without hesitation for about two and a half centuries.

On the basis of Newton's laws the forecasting of astronomical events continued. It was possible to know the position of a planet next week, next month, next year, etc. A number of calculations were done in this regard. On their basis, forecasting was done.

However, calculations based on Newton's law were not able to solve a set of mysteries. The rotation of planet Mercury is different and peculiar. It is also a small planet compared to other planets.

In Newton's era, it was believed that all planets and stars rotate about their axes and they also rotate around the sun. This phenomenon was considered a divine rule as all the religions believe that this has been created by God.

It was imagined that the space between planets and stars is 'Antariksha' and it is vacuum. All these planets and stars move in this space and they have got an absolute space which can be generally measured.

Similar concepts were developed for the daily activities of mankind. If somebody is performing yoga, he is considered at rest or zero speed while the speed of a moving train is considered say 60 km per hour.

But the reality is otherwise. In fact our earth is moving at a very high speed on its axis. This speed is not available at both the poles. Since the earth is moving around the sun at a very high speed, nothing at the poles is at absolute rest.

In due course, it was established that the sun is also not at rest. It is also moving. Since it is a gaseous sphere, its movement is not exactly as that of a planet but it is moving. At the same time, it is also moving on a definite path.

Thus, Albert presented the concept of relativity. He categorically stated that there is no absolute motion in the universe. All the motions are relative to others. Due to this, it is difficult to define any motion.

It can be explained this way: "When we go for boating, all the trees and plants situated on the bank of a river look mobile. But the fact is that the boat is mobile and in relation with this, the trees and plants look mobile, of course, in opposite direction."

Under this new concept, there can be several speeds of any object such that:

1. A car is moving at a speed of 5 metres per second with respect to the earth. This means this calculation is based while considering the earth stationary.
2. A car is moving at a speed of 30,000 metres per second. This speed is with respect to the sun i.e. the sun is considered stationary.
3. A car is moving at a speed of 2,50,000 metres per second. This speed is with respect to the centre of our galaxy.

All above statements are true. But this created turmoil in scientific society. Till that time, whatever calculations done were considered absolute. At that time, an imaginary material Ether was considered all around us. This hypothesis was also hurt very badly.

But Einstein was convinced by his own theory and declared that all the motions in the universe are relative and there is nothing absolute.

There was a change in the dimensions also. Till then, calculations were done in terms of kilometres per hour or metres per second. Now, a new basis was evolved, i.e. velocity of light denoted by C.

The light moves with a very high velocity. It is 10 million times faster than the speed of a common man. Time taken in putting on the shoes is enough for light to travel around the earth several times.

Einstein explained the importance of the velocity of light in his theory of relativity. He said, "While travelling by train, if a dish falls from your hands, it will fall at your feet only, whether the train is stationary or moving at any speed (normal nature). Under these circumstances, Newton's law is applied."

"If a sudden brake is applied or the train is moving on curved rails, the dish will not fall this way. It will fall differently." Under these circumstances, Newton's law will not be applied directly.

The situation will be quite peculiar if the train is moving like a wave.

With the above logics it can be concluded that there is no measurement procedure which can declare that a particular object is stationary or moving with a particular speed.

Einstein also developed a hypothesis that the velocity of light is maximum. This is 30,00,00,000 metres per second. In comparison to this all other speeds are negligible. For example, the speed of sound is just 330 metres per second. □

New Definition of Time

Man is able to experience speed, light and time. Some times, these experiences are real. For example, if we are moving in a car or a train, we are able to experience its speed.

Sometimes, these experiences can be imaginary also. Suppose you are travelling in a car and the car is moving with the speed of light. What will happen? You will reach planet Venus or Mars in a couple of minutes.

However, the experiences of both the travels will be quite different. While travelling by an ordinary car you enjoy yourself the scenes of journey. You see the trees, objects moving in opposite direction. If you travel in the car moving with the speed of light, you will not be able to see anything.

How is it possible? We are able to see everything when the light rays falling on an object reach our eyes. This is possible only when we travel with slow speed. If we travel with the speed of light, the rays falling on these objects will not be able to reach the eyes of the traveller and he will not be able to see anything outside.

However, it is also true that there is no measurement which can tell whether you are stationary or moving with a uniform speed. Till now, the basis of experience of movement is that we see the outer object moving in the opposite direction. If we move with the velocity of light, this method also fails. You will feel as if you were not moving.

Albert Einstein put forward another hypothesis. He said that the speed of light is absolute. A bowler starts running to throw a ball in cricket ground and his speed is 5 metres per second. He throws the ball with a speed of 10 metres per second. The real speed of the ball is 15 metres per second.

If the bowler after running flashes a torch instead of throwing a ball, the speed of flash light should be—the, bowlers speed + speed of light. But the fact is different. Whatever may be the speed of the bowler, the speed of light is the same.

This does not happen with the speed of sound. If we travel in the opposite direction from the source of sound, we can experience the difference in speed. Later on, when supersonic flights started, this effect was easily seen and experienced. We are not able to listen to the roar of their flight as they move at twice the speed of sound or even more.

This does not happen with light. Whether we travel by plane or in a rocket, the flash of the light travels with the same speed.

But the calculation of the speed of light is a cumbersome job. If we generate light from any of its source and it returns from any mirror, if the time duration of this is to be calculated, it is very difficult. For this, a suitable clock can be designed but with great difficulty.

By means of this clock if time taken in shaving is to be calculated it has to tick billion times.

In this regard, a hypothetical experiment will be beneficial by which we can develop better concept about the velocity of light. It is like this:

Your friend is standing with a light clock and you are concentrating on the light. In this situation, light appears as a bright point to you. The point will move up and down. When it strikes a mirror and comes down, then the time taken will be, say 1 nanosecond, the light clock ticks after this duration.

Now assume that your friend starts running and his speed is one-fourth of light. Now the movement of the light point will be like zigzag:

If your friend starts running faster than before, the shape of zigzag will change and will look like:

As a result, the zigzag will become longer which means: as the speed of your friend increases, the speed of light source will also be increased. This means the speed of light will remain the same but the above hypothetical light clock will take more time according to the speed of the runner.

This means time will be slower. Before arriving to any conclusion, three points are to be taken care of:

1. As regards the person running with the light clock, he is carrying the clock. He is seeing the clock ticking. He is seeing the light point moving up and down. For him, the clock is working with the same speed and giving the same time.

2. If the person running is standing before and playing yo-yo in which the ball tied with the string comes and goes from the hand, we can comfortably watch it as it has the duration of a few seconds.

   If the person playing yo-yo starts running, the yo-yo also will look like zigzag like the last figure. With whatever speed the man runs, the speed of yo-yo coming in the hand and going out of the hand will remain the same.

   If the man running moves much faster, then the speed of yo-yo will be faster, but it will not look so.

3. In this regard, there is one more fact that with speed time shrinks but the shrinkage rate is very small. If you keep your watch in a vehicle which moves continuously at a speed of 75 km per second, in a year there will be a time difference of one second only.

With this, a new concept was developed that the time becomes slower in moving vehicles. This means clocks, machines, body of drivers, thoughts of passengers, etc. all become slower in moving vehicles.

But the persons sitting in the vehicle will not be able to feel it. They will see or experience in relation to one another. Only the persons seeing from outside will be able to experience it.

With this, a new hypothesis was developed. According to this, if a person is sent in a rocket and if it is possible to watch his activities sitting here on the earth, we will find that:

1. As the speed of the rocket increases, the activities of the person will become slower.
2. If it is possible to move the rocket with the speed of light, we will find that the activities of the passenger will be standing still.
3. On the other hand, if it is possible for the person to watch the activities on the earth with telescope, then he will find that the activities are almost standstill. He will see the slower motion of flying birds. The flow of rivers will look like statues.

But the fact is that not only for man, but for planets or other celestial objects also, it is not possible to move with the speed of light.

The structure of the theory of relativity was ready, whose summary is as under:

1. Laws of nature remain the same whether the person is standstill or mobile.
2. It is impossible to ascertain whether one is stationary or moving with at a certain speed.
3. Speed of the light is the same. This speed is absolute.
4. Time becomes slower in a moving vehicle. The more is the speed of the vehicle, the slower becomes the time. Our brain also slows down.

5. If a person outside the vehicle sees the activities of the person travelling inside, he will find his activities slower.
6. Similarly, if the passenger travelling in the vehicle sees outside, he will also find outer activities slower.

□

Space-Time—New Relations

Einstein had proved that time slows in a moving vehicle. But the mathematical equation to define how much slow time becomes is quite lengthy and cumbersome. But this can be explained easily by this experiment.

A person has a light clock which is of one metre length. This means light travels a distance of one metre with a speed of 30 crore metre per second. This journey takes a time of 3.3 nanosecond. This is the minimum time because the light travels in a straight line.

If a person starts running taking this light clock, the distance covered by the light in new situation is more which can be understood by an illustration.

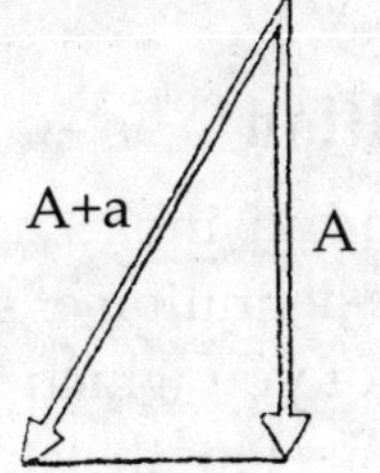

A + a = distance travelled by light when the person is running

A = Distance travelled by light when the person is at rest.

As the person increases his speed, the distance travelled by light (i.e. a) will also increase.

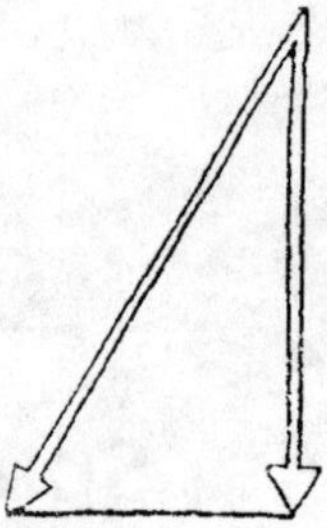

If we know the speed of the person running, we can calculate the change in time by the following equation:

Here, T = time (when the person is stationary)

S = speed of the person running

C = speed of the light

t = new time due to running

As explained earlier, if the person is running with half the speed light, the new time taken will be calculated like this:

$$t = \frac{T}{\sqrt{1 - \frac{S^2}{C^2}}}$$

= 3.8 nanosecond

This means if the person runs at half the speed of light, the difference in time is just .5 nanosecond. This means the speeds available in the world will have negligible impact on time. Even if the person runs at 90% of the speed of light, the difference per second is just 0.436 second, i.e. 43.6 per cent difference.

Space - new definition

Theory of Relativity had an impact not only on the definition of time but also on the definition of space. Suppose, there is a train coach in front of you which has a length 12 metres. When it is stationary, its length can be easily measured.

If the coach is moving with a high speed, one method of calculating its speed is that a person standing at one corner should fire with a gun ejecting a beam of rays. When these rays reach on the other side of the coach, the time duration should be calculated.

The rays ejected from the gun will travel with a speed of 300,000,000 metres per second. If the time duration is 0.00000004 second, it means

Length of the coach = speed of light × time taken in reaching from one end to other end
= 300,000,000 × 0.00000004
= 12 metres

If we measure by tape or by this method, the result will be 12 metres only. If the train is moving, the time taken in reaching from one end to other end will be different.

In this regard, Einstein gave a formula which is as under:

Length while moving = Normal length *i.e.* length while stationary × $\sqrt{1-\frac{S^2}{C^2}}$

If person is running with half the speed of light then the time taken by the clock will be $t = \dfrac{3.3}{1-\dfrac{150,000,000^2}{300,000,000^2}}$

Here also S = speed of train and C is speed of light

It is clear that the available speeds at the earth will not have any impact on length which can be felt. If any vehicle moves at a speed comparable with light, the length will change significantly.

The above process has an impact. When radiation enters from space, at the height of 10 kilometres from the surface of the earth, small micro particles Muons are generated.

These small particles have very low life and their total life span is a very small fraction of one second.

These particles take 0.000004 second in reaching the surface of the earth. This means their speed is

= 2,500,000,000 metres per second

But this speed is 8 times more than the speed of light. Hence, it is impossible.

According to the theory of Albert Einstein, if an object travels with a very high speed, the time becomes slower. These small micro-particles also travel with a comparable speed of light. Hence, their time becomes slower. If a clock is attached with 'Muons', it will show this fact.

Thus the following facts emerged by means of Theory of Relativity:

1. Every man can only say that he is moving with a particular speed with respect to a certain object.
2. If a man is travelling in a vehicle moving at a very high speed, his time becomes slower. An interesting fact is that the traveller finds your time slower.
3. Similarly, if a man travels in a vehicle moving at a high speed, his space shrinks. Here also, an interesting fact is that the traveller feels that the space of outer man or outer space is shrinking.
4. Hence, a statement that two events are occurring simultaneously at different places is not safe. It can be wrong also.

□

Fourth Dimension

As soon as the relativity theory was put forward and a new definition of space and time was developed, turmoil started in the scientific world. The people, who used to ignore Einstein, now started giving deep thought to various statements given by him. A number of discussions started at various places and at various levels.

One of the teachers Albert Hermann Minco wski while teaching Einstein was convinced that this lazy dog would not do anything, at least, in mathematics.

When the relativity theory developed by Einstein came to his knowledge, it was a pleasant surprise for him. He not only studied it but he also started giving lectures on it. During this period, a search for fourth dimension started. Till then, the space and time were having separate entities. Now, they were related to each other.

Now, they were popular as space-time.

Before the arrival of Einstein on the scientific forum, three dimensions were known to the world. These were:

1. Up-down
2. Left-Right
3. Backward-Forward (or near and far)

If we see from other angle, the following analysis emerges.

Suppose we don't have one of the above three dimensions. We shall be having only the following options:

Up-down

Left-right

Combination of the both

This means that the world will become a piece of paper in which two dimensional maps will be inserted. This situation can be explained practically also. For example, if we make a narrow horizontal slit in a big piece of cardboard by blade and then see, we shall be able to see only left and right. We shall also be able to see near and far. We shall not be able to see up and down.

If the above situation really happens, every man will become like a flat picture. He will not be able to see the world as he sees it today. He will try to see the other person from various angles and try to touch also till he is confident about his real existence.

This kind of situation arises in daily life also and we don't become confident about many things just by seeing them. As it can be imagined that a man of two dimensional worlds can imagine about the third dimension, the persons of this world also can imagine about the fourth dimension. Both of them can't see the additional dimension.

Now, we again go to the world of two dimensions and take a tile. Slowly, we start pressing more and we find the impressions in the following manner, *i.e.* lines will first increase and then decrease.

Seeing these lines the persons of two-dimensional world will find themselves under a mystery. They first increase and then decrease and ultimately vanish. The persons of two dimensional world, i.e. like flat pictures will definitely imagine that this is due to the third dimension only.

Imagine that there is a fourth dimension also. We shall not be able to see this dimension as the persons like flat pictures are not able to see the third dimension. If we

press a four-dimensional object on a paper or cardboard, we shall also get an impression, i.e. size will first increase and then decrease and ultimately, it will vanish.

The fact is that in our real life, we mostly see the two dimensional objects. We first have a two-dimensional image in our brain. We assess about the third dimension from these two dimensional pictures only.

Its glaring example is: generally, we see a wild animal like lion on television and get afraid when we find if approaching us. But the reality is that television screen is just two dimensional. But the changes in this make us experience the third dimension.

Similarly, when we see a cube and become curious to see it from below, we shall find it as a flat square and it becomes difficult to assess what it is.

Albert Einstein and Hermann Minkowski had a lengthy discussion on the issue of the fourth dimension. Minkowski imagined that this fourth dimension is time. Till then, we were familiar with the three dimensions of space and Einstein had already made the world acquainted with the new definition of time and its relation with space.

People started imagining about four dimensions with respect to space-time. In this regard, the following experiment can be studied.

A man is standing in the sun with a javelin in his hand. His image is reaching the earth in the form of shadow which is two dimensional. If the position of the javelin is changed, the length of the shadow will change. But the reality is that the real length of the javelin remains as it is. If the javelin is moved with a very high speed, we shall experience decrease in length of the javelin.

If this javelin is one metre long and it is thrown at the speed equivalent to 90% of the speed of light, there will be a change in its length. If it is measured with the previous formula of Einstein,

$$\text{Moving length} = \text{Normal length} \times \sqrt{1 - \frac{S^2}{C^2}}$$

Its length will be just 14 centimetres. This means the faster is the javelin, the shorter is the javelin.

If there are people in this world who are having several eyes and they are capable of seeing several dimensions (at least the fourth one), they can see the javelin from various angles and will not think about shortening or increasing of its length.

Another method to understand this phenomenon is that the person should also move with the same speed as the javelin is being thrown.

Einstein gave the fourth dimension to the world which was based on time. Subsequently, the management professionals started using this time dimension for the display of the profits of the company. They were displaying it on paper only which is two dimensional.

Time-space again got interlinked by this fourth dimension. The theory of relativity was once again proved according to which the length of an object depends on its speed.

□

General Theory of Relativity

Einstein had proved with the help of relativity that it is impossible to prove that whether an object is absolutely stationary or moving (at what absolute speed).

Einstein kept on thinking in this direction. One day, he put forward one more hypothesis before the world that a man falling from a height will not feel the gravitational field.

Subsequently, this experience was needed when it was planned to send cosmonauts into space. In order to train them for weightlessness, they were advised to travel in the planes which first fly at a great height and then they suddenly dive. While diving, they feel the weightlessness quite clearly.

Similar is the experience of the persons moving in a lift. While coming down if the cable of the lift is disconnected, the lift will suddenly come down and the person inside will find himself, or the luggage in his hand, as light as a feather.

Einstein again developed a hypothesis according to which gravitation and acceleration are alike. Gravitation can be substituted for acceleration and vice-versa.

At the same time, it is also clear that the laws of physics are the same whether the person is mobile or not. For example, whether train is stationary, moving with a uniform speed or stopping by sudden brake, the laws of physics will remain the same.

When we travel in a particular vehicle and its speed increases or decreases, we feel it. We are able to experience acceleration as we experience gravitational force.

Einstein also put forward a hypothesis according to which the gravitational force affects light. Due to this, the light rays become curved. This was experimentally proved during the observations done at the time of Solar Eclipse.

Time Stops

Imagine a ball made up of furs is coming in a straight line. If you try to stop or catch it, you may not be able to do so. In this process, some of its furs will come into your hand. At the same time, due to your attempt, there will be a change in its direction.

Similar phenomenon is observed when the light rays reach an object having a strong gravitational field like the sun. At the same time, another fact emerges that these rays become slower.

A fact emerges that time becomes slower due to gravitational force. The gravitational force of the sun is considerably large as compared to that of the earth. It is so large that if a normal man reaches the sun and measures his weight, he will find it one and a half ton.

Even then, this huge gravitational force also puts negligible impact on the light. Due to this, the impact of time is also low. It makes time slower by one minute in a year.

But there are a number of objects in the universe whose gravitational force is very high. It is so high that the light sticks to it and disappears. These objects are black holes. They not only make time slower but make it almost stop. They stop the time in the same manner as catching the ball made up of furs.

If it is possible to have a vehicle on which we can sit and go to the black hole and a telescope is available with the help of which it is possible to see clearly the activities of the vehicle, we will find the moment this vehicle reaches near black hole, the activities of the persons sitting inside will become slower. The clock inside this will tick quite slowly. If the man resides on this black hole, he will spend extremely little time there as compared to the earth.

In this regard, an example can be given to explain it. If your parents leave for black hole during your childhood and spend some time there and return, they will remain younger. During that period at the earth, you will become old and you will welcome your parents with a bent back and a stick in hand. A broad estimate is available in this regard that one week there is equivalent to 20 years on the earth.

In our Puranas, there are descriptions related to time. One day of Brahma, one day of Devaraj Indra and one day on the earth are altogether different. Maybe, this is due to difference in gravitational force of Brahma Lok, Indra Lok and the earth. Similarly, persons like Narad Muni who would move constantly with very high speed, remained young in every era, i.e. Sat Era, Treta Era, Dwapar Era, etc. Probably, their time became quite slow.

According to the new definition of time developed by Einstein, a man can go in the past and will also be able to go into the future. Similar imagination is in Indian mythology also. Maharishi Valmiki had written the Ramayana, years before the birth of Lord Rama.

Mystery of Spinning

Imagine a wheel is spinning at a very high speed. It has already been proved that the objects moving at a high speed shrink. If the wheel moves with the speed equivalent to the speed of light, it will shrink. The diameter of the wheel reduces. If there are spokes in it like a bicycle wheel, they will also spin but the direction will be different. They will become thinner. Here an anomaly develops. The diameter of the wheel reduces but the length of the spoke remains the same. How is it possible.

With the help of his general theory of relativity, Einstein put forward his hypothesis that with the increase of speed time becomes slower and the space becomes curved.

This was immediately explained. For example the light rays or moving objects generally move in a straight line. If a planet or other object comes in between, there is a curve in the space time due to the mass of the object. This is similar to a train moving in a curved path.

The above situation can be explained in this way. If you are standing on the seashore and you have dug a pit around you, the ball coming towards you will move on a curved path.

How much curved it will be. To know this, complex mathematical equations will be required. Till then, the

Newton's laws were prevailing, which were quite simple such as:

$$P = mf$$

These were not giving the correct results. Einstein gave mathematical equations but they were not for common use. With their use, the anomalies regarding the path of planet Mercury ended.

Thus the general Theory of Relativity came forward clearly. Its summary is as under:

1. With the special Theory of Relativity it was only known that it is impossible to know that we are absolutely stationary or mobile with a particular speed. Now, it is also clear that we are not sure whether we are moving with acceleration or not. The explanation of gravitational force was difficult with the help of special theory of relativity.
2. With this new theory, Einstein proved that the gravitational force and acceleration are alike. This means that gravitational force has the same effect as the acceleration has and vice-versa.
3. Due to acceleration, the light rays move on a curved path. Hence, the gravitational force should also have the same effect.
4. If the path of light-rays becomes curved due to gravitational force, the light will also become slower.
5. This means the light clock will tick slower due to gravitational force.
6. Accordingly, gravitational force will make time slower.
7. As per the special theory of relativity, if the rim/tyre/ or wheel is moving with a high speed, the rim/tyre will shrink but the length of the spokes will remain the same. This is possible. They become so curved that

their additional length will not become a problem. This also means that rotation which is possible due to acceleration also makes the space curved.

8. Whatever is possible due to acceleration is also possible due to gravitational force. Thus, gravitational force also makes the space curved.
9. Gravitational force makes space-time curved.

□

Experimentally Proved

Understanding Einstein's theories in a correct way is difficult even today. During his period, the public mentality was altogether different. People including scientists were quite prejudiced. It was not easy to prove his theories to them experimentally.

One way of verification was to observe the light rays coming from other stars. They should look curved when they are near the sun. During normal days, it is difficult to observe the sun.

In this regard, the indirect method is to see the stars near the sun in a different place in the absence of the sun. This is possible only when there is solar eclipse.

At that time, the circumstances were equally difficult as were the equations of Einstein. During the solar eclipse of 1914, the First World War had started and the experiment was not possible.

It was calculated that another solar eclipse would be in 1919. To examine this hypothesis, two scientists' teams were constituted. One was led by Sir Arthur Eddington who was a prominent British scientist and was also a pacifist as was Einstein. He also refused to do war related research for his country during the First World War. This team reached a small island near West African coastal area to see the scenario of solar eclipse.

Another expedition team went to a place known as Sebral to see the same scenario. The reason was that if there were sudden clouds at the first place, verification could be done at the second place.

The photographs were taken on this occasion. After the event, the scientists were eager to see the photograph but the photography was not much developed during those days. The first four photographs were not fit for using as evidence. But the last photograph was very clear. The scientists got relief. This photo was clearly showing the position of stars different from normal days. This is due to the fact that the light coming from these stars bends a bit due to the gravitational force of the sun. As a result, one can see their different positions on the earth.

□

Expanding Universe

How did this universe evolve? How did it develop? What its future will be? A number of such questions had been raised often since ancient time. Several philosophers gave their views in this regard from time to time but no serious effort was made to verify these views or principles.

Nobody before Einstein took this subject so seriously. Whatever research was done by Newton, on the basis of that, it was believed that the universe is full of stars and this exists endlessly in space. In believing this theory, there was a problem in explaining a number of facts and events.

Till that time, it was also believed that the universe is created by God and it has been as such since creation. The following points existed in this regard:

1. These stars can be mobile continuously in various directions. But there was a problem in this. Since there are innumerable stars, there should be infinite gravitational force in all the directions. But it is not like this.
2. Although space is on all sides, yet the stars are in a

limited space. This means that our universe is like a small island in this infinite space. But this also has a problem. If the speed of the stars continues like this, there will be time when these stars will be out of sight.

Einstein kept on thinking in this direction. He had already proved that the objects like stars are really curved. If there are lakhs of stars in the sky, what will happen? In fact, their space will be more curved.

This clearly means that even if we continuously travel across the space, we will not find its end. If a powerful light-beam is sent in space, it will travel across entire space and reach the same point from where it was started.

With the help of his general Theory of Relativity, Einstein gave a complex equation to express the shape and size of the universe. But it had a peculiar constant. It was designated 'cosmological constant' by Einstein. But that one was also a puzzle which was solved.

According to Albert, all the stars attract through their gravitational force. It seems as if they were tied with stretched elastic.

To understand this, an experiment can be done. You wear an elastic tie and stretch it to the maximum. You can put a pie on the other end of the tie. Try to stretch it further. You will be able to pull it further with an upper limit of the length of arm.

In this way, Einstein's theory can be explained. In the above circumstances, the pie is one star and your face is another star. Elastic force is gravitational force and your arm's length is cosmological constant.

Other aspect of this is that the constant of Albert Einstein's formula is playing an important role. If it is not there or is loose, the pie will come back and strike at your face, i.e. the universe can shrink.

The above explanation was well taken by the then scientists' world but Einstein was not at all satisfied. He wanted the simplest theory which was easy to understand as well as to explain.

He took 12 years to arrive at his conclusions. In that era, a popular astronomer, Edwin Hubble, was also investigating and trying to know the limit of our universe. As per Einstein's formulae, the universe is expanding. But Hubble didn't have strong evidence in favour of this fact. Very soon, Hubble was convinced of the outcome of Einstein's observation done with his telescope. He found that the universe is really expanding. Despite this, the gravitational force is so strong that the universe is intact.

But the controversy on cosmological constant continued. Einstein took the help of his general Theory of Relativity. He insisted that one can't find the end of the universe even if he keeps on going farther in the universe. He tried to explain the shape of the universe with the help of the theory of curved space. There was a problem in this. Since all the stars attract one another by way of gravitational force, there is a strong probability that, one day, the universe will collapse. But Einstein also explained that there is an invisible force also which is generating a repulsive force due to which the stars are maintaining distance from one another.

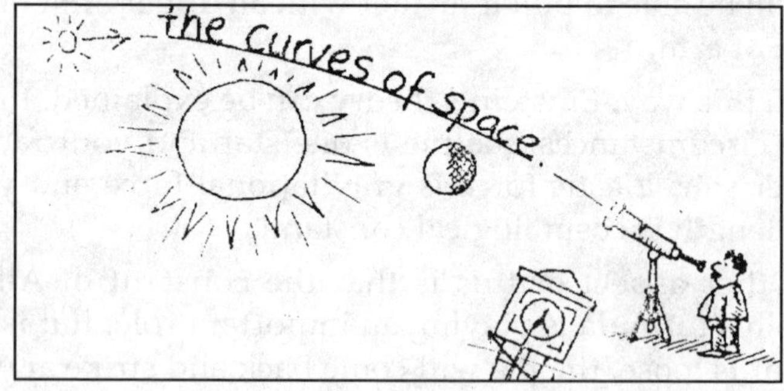

□

Disastrous Implementation of $E = mC^2$

Special Theory of Relativity

Einstein had proved that as the speed of the object increases and comes nearer to the speed of light, the time and space related to this get affected in a wonderful manner. The size of the object starts becoming smaller and the time becomes slower. This clearly means that if a clock is attached with this, it will move slower.

If the object starts moving with the speed equivalent to the speed of light, the clock will stop and the length of object will become zero.

However, the above concept can be considered imaginary, as achieving such a high speed is almost impossible. Einstein also put forward a hypothesis that no object can attain a speed higher than the speed of light.

Suppose you take a sand particle and throw it at the speed equivalent to 90% of the speed of light. What will happen? This speed is 30,00,00,000 times the speed of an average cricket bowler. When the sand particle collides with a wall with this speed, a big sound will be generated.

If you throw the same sand particle with double the effort, you will assume that this will collide with the wall

at the speed equivalent to 180 per cent of the speed of light. But this will not happen like this as the time becomes slower and the real speed of the particle will be only 97.2 per cent of the speed of light. But the sound generated will be very high. The wall may shake and it will have many cracks.

If you throw the ball with the effort equivalent to 20 times of original effort the real speed of the particle will be 99.97 per cent of the speed of light. When that sand particle collides with the wall at this speed, it will smash not only the wall but the entire building.

This can be interpreted in another way also. When an

object moves with an extraordinary speed, it becomes quite heavy. We experience in our daily life also that we feel hurt when the object colliding is either heavy or travelling at a high speed. If a light ball or heavy ball collides with us at the same speed, the heavy ball hurts more.

Above analysis enables us to conclude: while throwing, the energy inducted makes its speed not only higher but heavier also.

In this regard, an equation emerges:

mobile mass =

$$\text{mobile mass} = \frac{\text{Normal Mass}}{\sqrt{1 - \frac{S^2}{C^2}}}$$

Here, S is the speed of the object.

Einstein discovered a new relation between mass and energy. A new equation emerged:

$E = mC^2$

It was concluded that a piece of matter is equivalent to certain amount of energy. To calculate this, the mass of the object is to be multiplied by square of the speed of light.

Since the speed of light is very high, the square of this is further high. Thus a small particle can also generate a huge amount of energy.

This also means that if the energy equivalent to a sand particle is available, it can heat water kept in one crore kettles.

A number of facts were collected in favour of the above hypothesis. For example, if a fuel, say wood, is burnt and we take the weight of ash and smoke, the difference in original fuel and the residue is not much. But a small portion of matter creates enough amount of energy. The sun, whose centre is under tremendous pressure, keeps on sending sufficient amount of energy in solar system.

On the other hand, energy can also be converted into any form of matter. We see that sunlight falls on a growing plant. Along with sun light, carbon dioxide and moisture are bound. Due to this, the development of plants is accelerated. Additional matter is generated such as flowers and fruit. The mass of fruit is more than the carbon dioxide and moisture. This clearly means that the additional mass generated is due to light energy. When human beings, animals and birds eat these fruits, the same is reconverted to energy. Thus, a sequence of the conversion of energy continues in nature.

The proposed equation of Einstein E= mc2 means—

1. When the energy is locked at one place, it is converted to matter.
2. When it is released, it restarts working as energy.

This means every particle of matter is having a huge amount of energy in hidden form as C^2 is having a very large value.

Einstein wrote an article elaborating the above concept in 1920. He explained, "If the matter is broken at micro level, i.e. atomic level, a lot of energy will be released. If this released energy starts breaking the other atoms, a chain of reaction will start and a source of huge amount of energy will be built up."

This process is just like the process in a bicycle stand. The bicycles are parked in a row. If one bicycle pushed, the second, the third and so on will start falling. This process will continue till the last bicycle.

This is the process that forms the basis of an atom bomb. If the process of nuclear fission starts, it will continue till the last atom. Einstein got puzzled as to how to start this chain. He could not find a clue for this till 1935.

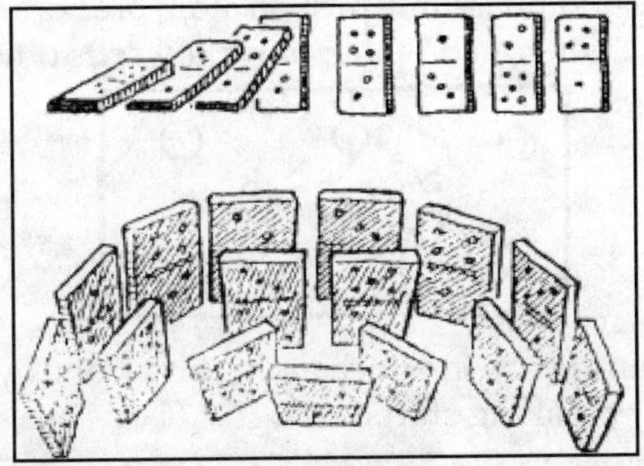

Einstein had an interest in theoretical physics and he never wanted to build atomic power. He never had an interest in the atomic politics which was beginning to raise its head.

But time and tide never wait. Several scientists in several countries, based on Theory of Relativity, had started research in this direction.

On January 27, 1939, famous scientist Niels Bohr, disclosed in a conference at Washington that a German scientist Otto Hahn, a former colleague of Einstein, had achieved success in breaking the atom. He also informed the conference that apart from a huge amount of energy as a result of the process, barium was also created. The scientists present in the conference were shocked and could visualise a powerful future atom bomb capable of generating disaster.

Initial hypothesis was like as shown below:

The first phase in which a particle approaches an atom.

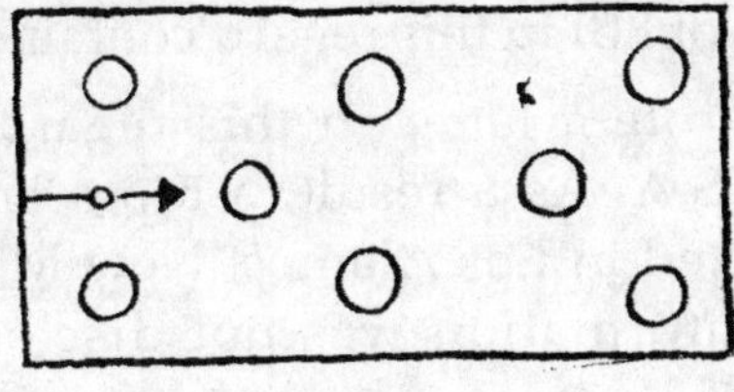

The second phase in which an atom breaks and several particles are generated which move towards other atoms.

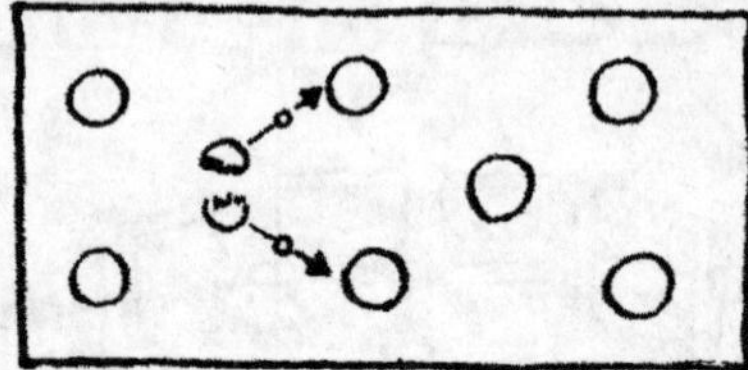

The third phase in which atoms break one by one. The sequence of breaking starts.

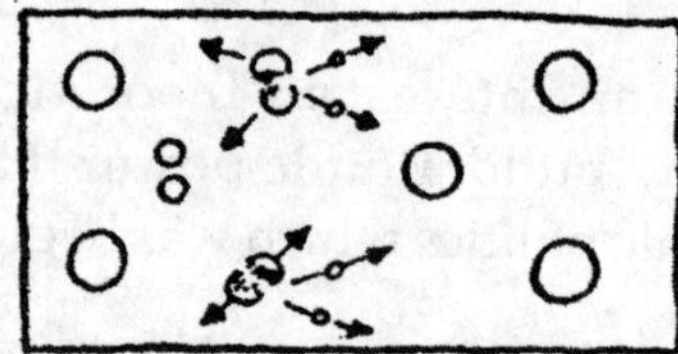

For this process, the need for proper material was felt, which should be radioactive. U235 was considered an ideal material for this.

Politics started for U235 at the world level. Germany instructed Czechoslovakia not to sell Uranium to Russia. On the other hand, Einstein was requested to use his relations with the Royal family of Belgium and prevent Belgium so that it might not sell Congolese uranium to Germany. At that time, Congo had a huge reserve of uranium and it was under the dominion of Belgium.

In this situation, the credibility of Einstein increased considerably in the U.S. Earlier, because of his pacifism, he was under the close observation of FBI, a secret agency of the U.S. The file of FBI in this regard contained 1427 pages.

Einstein wrote a letter in this regard to President Roosevelt of U.S.A. As a result, a top secret Manhattan project was started in Los Alamos, New Mexico, in 1941. Initially, this information was not disclosed to Albert

Einstein. However, he would always come to know of things. A number of top scientists had disappeared around the time and some of them were his old friends. They used to consult with him regarding this project also.

Finally, Einstein was fully involved in this war related research and kept on giving various kinds of scientific advice to American Navy.

The first result came on 6th August 1945 when an atom bomb was dropped at Hiroshima. 78,150 persons died instantly. A kilometre wide area was converted to sheer ground. Einstein had already visited Hiroshima in 1925.

Subsequently, lots of people died in both the cities. In addition to this, a large number of people became injured and finally disabled.

□

Efforts for Super Science

(Grand Unified Theory)

All the theories described so far were developed by Einstein during 1905-27. He died in 1955. People generally believe that he spent rest of his life, *i.e.* 28 years studying Judaism, Pacifism and research on explosives, bombs, etc. during the Second World War. But this is a half truth.

In 1928, his heart problem became severe and he was confined to bed for four months. He utilised his bed-rest for thinking.

During this process, he evaluated his work done so far and found that:

1. He had developed the special theory of relativity.
2. He had developed the general theory of relativity.
3. He had contributed to the development of Quantum Theory.
4. He had developed the theory of light.
5. He had proved that the space and time are interlinked.

6. He had also proved that the matter and energy are convertible to each other.

7. Gravitation and acceleration are alike.

In spite of proving various interlinked things/theories, Einstein was not satisfied. He developed another hypothesis and said that electricity, magnetism and gravitation force are either same or interlinked.

Though he was involved in the development of Quantum Theory, yet he was not satisfied with its outcome—everything in the universe is fuzzy and it can't be defined exactly.

Magnetism had been a favourite subject for Einstein since childhood when he was presented a compass to play with. Apart from this, when he developed the general Theory of Relativity, he was keen to explain the various incidences about the universe.

With the passage of time, Einstein's method of working also changed. Earlier, he was not using mathematics so extensively. He used it for giving generality to the theories or filling the blanks in it. Later on, mathematics became his main tool. He wanted to use it for developing a new model of the universe. By doing so, he hoped that the real shape of the universe would emerge and the remaining mysteries, which were confusing the scientists, would be solved.

As per the imagination of Einstein, the universe was having a very simple structure. He hoped that he would be able to explain electricity and magnetism also in the same way as he had shown through relativity theory that gravity is curvature of space-time. Every theory/process will have one or similar theory only.

Einstein named his proposed theory as Grand Unified Theory. He desired that a set of equations should be developed, which should be applicable to all kinds of forces.

Einstein continued to work on his hypothesis throughout his life but to no purpose. During post-Einstein era, this research continued. In this regard, a super string theory was developed. But everything could not be explained through this theory.

□

Social Philosophy of Albert Einstein

Scientist Einstein also gave deep thoughts to various social issues and expressed his views before the world on numerous occasions. These thoughts were kept either in the form of lectures or in the form of written statements or letters. These were compiled. The abstract of his social philosophy is produced below:

Science and Values

According to Einstein, human interest should get the highest priority while developing science and technology. Generally, scientists become so engressed in their work that they forget even themselves while designing drawings, equations, etc. Under no circumstances, they should forget the human interests.

He also said that whatever creative work is done in the area of science should be such that it should benefit humanity. He believed that a life spent for others is the only useful life.

During the fag end of the Einstein era, a number of questions were raised over the atom bomb, atomic energy and its control. Einstein had a definite and important role in the development of this bomb. There were very many apprehensions about its future use. Many people believed that Einstein had contributed to the construction of a highly destructive thing, which might destroy this whole world as well as humanity.

However, Einstein was still optimistic. He didn't see any point in the statement that the whole humanity would be annihilated due to this. At the most if the atom bombs would be used on a large scale, two-third of human population would be destroyed. Even then, a large number of people would survive and sufficient books having plenty of knowledge would survive and human civilization would again develop and regain its shape.

At that time, a kind of war was going on. Scientists and intellectuals were in dilemma. They were feeling that they were not heard and the politicians were working at their own whims.

But Einstein was confident. He believed, "If intellectuals participate in the political struggle, they will not succeed. They can play effective role by putting their clear views about the situation and implementing successful strategies. They can give knowledge and wisdom to politicians so that they may act without prejudices."

Einstein himself created examples by putting his clear views from time to time. The biggest event of his era was atomic power and control over it. He put forward his views as chairman of the committee of nuclear scientists. He said, "Today, this nuclear power is with those who don't know whether to use it for better purpose or worse one. Hence, a new kind of thinking is required so that humanity may see new heights."

He used to emphasize the court of wisdom. He believed, "If this is established, powerful decision will be taken on moral grounds. Inner consciousness of man will prevail and establish standards in the social and economic affairs."

The above concepts of Einstein were not just hypothetical. He also explained the process of establishing such type of courts at Harvard. On the occasion of the third centenary of University, he gave a lecture and said that the court would have the best brains. In a letter written in 1939, he mentioned that the intellectual powers and spiritual powers of the world should unite together. This unified power would act like the soul of humanity.

He had great faith in intellectual power. He also felt that political power should also come to those people who were intellectually bright. Hence, all the intellectual people should unite. Even if the intellectuals of the free world were united, the hostile attitude of the politicians would be controlled. Not only this unity of intellectuals would provide a basis for the majority public to think but co-operation on various issues at international level would also start. If this work started, the intellectual community would gain an opportunity to do a big and historic service to the society.

Einstein also commented on the non-alignment of the scientists. He said, "When a scientist works in his laboratory, he works objectively. How can he remain vague on the issues of national importance? Every scientist has to act as a scholar as well as a civilian."

On the occasion of the birthday celebration of the former American President Abraham Lincoln, Einstein wrote a letter that the scientists should act in unison. They should have full freedom of teaching and publishing their research. If there was a ban on their research or their teaching, they should protest. He had an apprehension that the government would either ban or control the teachers' activities by economic sanction or by using money power. Hence, preventive measures were essential.

State and Individual

Einstein had a clear opinion that the individual should not do anything against his inner consciousness, whatever be the pressure from the state, the government or the administration.

Einstein accepted the responsibilities of an individual towards state but also said that the individual should evaluate his deeds from time to time. At the same time, one should be responsible to God first instead of being responsible to any individual.

He explained with examples the individual's dilemma, when to satisfy the state, he has to do good or bad. In fact, he should follow duties first before following the rules framed by the state. Whenever there is a conflict between man's duty and desires of state, the individual should act as per his own duties and conscience. On such occasions, the inner consciousness is the best judge and guiding force.

During his era, various kinds of trials were going on in various countries. The trials of Nuremberg were quite famous. Einstein considered these trials as the mockery of justice. He said, "The judges sitting during these trials are killing their conscience just for some money or due to pressure and they are needlessly pleasing the state."

He also said, that "There is a distinct difference between an individual and the society. If the state commits mistake under the pressure of an individual, it should also be evaluated."

Pacifism, Bomb and Ban on Wars

Einstein was a strong pacifist for most part of his life. He was dead against militarisation. However, when fascism started, he felt that it could be dealt with military action only.

He agreed to an extent to the Satyagraha, the non-violent mass movement started by Mahatma Gandhi. He also felt, "If the other side is militarily stronger and not ready to listen to others, it can be dealt with military action only." He was confident that Nazism would destroy the human civilization. To combat this, violent military action was essential.

When atom bomb was developed to deal with Nazism, the world got a new branch of science now known as Atomic Science. He decided this should be owned by the whole world. For this a World Government was essential, which would save the humanity. Now rivalries were to be finished and co-operation enhanced. The thinking and methods adopted till date could not avoid the world wars. A new thinking was essential which could avoid wars. Since the U.S. was ahead in the process of atomic power, he had to act with more responsibility.

He also said, "The defence mechanism for this atomic power is not of classical nature. This weapon can't be dealt with a similar weapon. This new science can create destruction but can't act as a saviour. We can't avoid it by being underground. We can avoid this situation by only maintaining the law and order tightly."

"We should do continuous evaluation of a foreign policy and ensure that it is not driving us to anarchy or death." He desired that the methods of constructing a bomb should not be left open. "Since both man and science are free, they will not remain confidential. This problem is not related to physics. This deals with ethics. Hence no solution will be found with the help of unnecessary rules and regulations. It is easier to destroy plutonium from Nature rather than to destroy evils inside man."

Till his last breath, Einstein kept on talking about forming the World Government. He was fully confident about this concept. He used to advise people to move above narrow nationalism. He used to emphasize on making United Nations stronger. He also desired that this should play a major role in educational uplift so that so-called backward countries might progress.

Einstein was dead against dropping of atom bombs on Hiroshima and Nagasaki. Many people argued, "If the atom bombs were not used, the Japanese would not have conceded defeat." In reply to this, Einstein said, "If at all dropping bomb was essential, it should have been dropped on a barren land away from population. Having seen its impact, the Japanese might have surrendered." In that era, people had a lot of apprehensions about atom bomb and its impact. However, Einstein opined that people should know more and more about it and this was the only remedy.

He believed that atom bomb was a threat not only to the politicians or generals of army but also to the whole humanity. The information about its impact should reach rural areas also. "In order to solve a social problem, it is essential to develop a social concept about it. In fact, the real problem is inside human minds."

Einstein also gave a deep thought about future relations between Russia and America. According to him, "Today's Russia is altogether different than yesterday's Germany. Its vision is also different. In Nazi Germany, the intellectuals, their creations and products were either opposed or destroyed. On the other hand, there is nothing of this kind in Russia. However, he was feeling that the nationalism was rising in Russia rapidly. At that time, he was not able to believe that the working freedom of intellectuals was being hurt.

He was annoyed at the excess of nationalism. He also believed that the feeling of nationalism was more in the U.S.A. than in Russia. Till his last breath, he hated mob violence.

At that time, the communists were considered untouchables in the U.S.A. People even used to maintain distance from them while travelling in buses, trains and airplanes. But Einstein was unaffected in this environment. He never did any kind of discrimination with any communist.

Apart from this, he was a member of a number of such organizations, which were considered communist. He even advocated for them from time to time.

Einstein had a deep rooted sympathy towards the minorities. He also used to jump into the activities which were considered unpopular. In many cases, he went too far. Several authors used to write differently from contemporary trends. So, they would face stiff opposition. Einstein used to side with them strongly. An author named Henry Wallace created a new kind of book, focusing on world peace. It created an uproar but Einstein supported him.

Einstein felt, "America is unnecessarily developing enmity with Russia. Soviet Russia is far behind America, both in production power and military power, America is far superior to Russia. Under present circumstances, the U.S.A. is more responsible for world disturbance. It should do more efforts to put back the world's situation on right track."

He also said that more powerful nations should have different kinds of responsibilities. At the same time, they should create examples of Ethics also. They should act more politely and use more wisdom. "This is possible when we rise above narrow nationalism."

Till his last days, Einstein kept on advocating for World Government. He felt that humanity could be fully secured only when its responsibility would rest on the shoulders of a World Government.

□

Judaism

Einstein's religious philosophy was not different from his social philosophy. He also considered Judaism quite relevant.

He believed that Jewish religion laid emphasis on morality. This is not a different kind of religion. This negates superstition. This is based on ethical values. It is like a way of life. It emphasizes on purity of life.

Einstein also said that the world, particularly the West, has gained a lot from Jewish religion. This religion has given a variety of moral education to the whole world. He also believed that the concept of socialism was initiated by this religion only.

Einstein had a clear concept of God. He believed that the existence of God can be very well seen in the homogeneity of the world, which is like a fabric. He said that he does not believe in a God which only keeps the record of deeds and fates of individuals.

Einstein used to believe in unity. He also believed that there is only one God. He kept his views about God and religion from time to time before the world. He also imagined about the evolution of religion in ancient time. When the social status of life was uplifted, the moral level of mankind also improved. Afterwards, the religion took a shape which has been prevailing even today.

He also believed that the aims and objectives of Judaism are not political. They are, in fact, social and cultural. According to him, Palestine is not just an asylum of Jewish refugees living here and there for two millennia. It is a sacred place for reviving the Jewish nation. Its first step should be to develop honour and tolerance for each other. Then only can a separate identity of the Jews survive. They will be able to maintain their healthy existence. Subsequently, they will gain essential dignity.

However, this is not sufficient. If the Jews have to participate in the cultural development of civilization, the nation for the Jews is to be established and it has to fulfill its duties. Today, it is our responsibility that we should actively participate in the economic and cultural reconstruction of our original nation.

Thus, Einstein had proved that he was not a mere scientist. He was an intellectual who wanted to fulfill his duties as a citizen and also leave an example for others to follow.

□

The Magnificent Jew

"Science without religion is lame, and religion without science is blind,"—that often repeated statement is attributed to Einstein. By his own definition, Einstein was a deeply religious man.

His Jewish background and upbringing were significant to him. His Jewish identity was strong and kept on widening as he grew older. His concept of God corresponded to that of the Jewish philosopher, Spinoza. Certainly, in his adult life, he was no synagogue-attending traditional follower of Judaism. But it is accurate enough to call his religious affiliation 'Jewish.'

In 1929, the scientist told Rabbi Herbert S. Goldstein, "I believe in Spinoza's God who reveals himself in the lawful harmony of the world, not in a God who concerns Himself with the fate and the doings of mankind."

Most sources indicate that he did not clearly believe in a personal god. When he talked about God, he was speaking in a more Spinozan sense. He was not speaking of a strictly Judeo-Christian Biblical conception of God. He wrote, his belief is a noble 'cosmic religious feeling' that enables scientists to advance human knowledge.

"The most beautiful and profound emotion we can experience is the sensation of the mystical. It is the source of all true science. He, to whom this emotion is a stranger, who can no longer wonder and stand rapt in awe, is as good as dead. To know what is impenetrable to us, really exists, manifesting itself as the highest wisdom and the most radiant beauty, which our dull faculties can comprehend only in their primitive forms, this knowledge, this feeling, is at the centre of true religion," he wrote.

Pacifism and supra-nationalism were the two main political ideals of this German born theoretical physicist. In the 1920s, he supported universal disarmament and a united Europe. After the Second World War, he championed the concept of World Government and the peaceful and only the peaceful uses of atomic energy.

The Nazi rise to power in Germany and its armed might have motivated Einstein to persuade the United States to build its own atomic weapons which ultimately led to the dropping of bombs on Japan. He realized the danger posed to humanity by atomic weapons and began campaigning for peace in the world with the help of other scientists of his time. During the last decade of his life, he was tireless in his efforts to bring about international co-operation to prevent war.

Einstein is, undoubtedly, one of the most fascinating and influential figures of the twentieth century. As a physicist, he radically transformed our understanding of the universe. As a humanist, he took active interest in the issues of his times and was concerned about peace and progress of humankind. He was outspoken about the political and social developments of his times. In the confrontation between

Nazism and Zionism, he advocated the Jewish cause and highlighted the dangers posed by Germany's military and economic strength.

He was notable not only for his scientific achievements but also for great humanistic philosophy. The world as he saw it could be summarized thus in his own words, "How strange the lot of us (mortals) is! Each of us is here for a brief sojourn; for what purpose he knows not, though he sometimes thinks yet he senses it. But without deeper reflection one knows from daily life that one exists for other people — first of all, for those upon whose smiles and well-being our own happiness is wholly dependent, and then for the many, unknown to us, to whose destinies we are bound by the ties of sympathy. A hundred times every day I remind myself that my inner and outer life are based on the labours of other men, living and dead, and that I must exert myself in order to give in the same measure as I have received and am still receiving".

"I have never looked upon ease and happiness as ends in themselves—this critical basis I call the ideal of a pigsty. The ideals that have lighted my way and time after time have given me new courage to face life cheerfully, have been kindness, beauty, and truth. Without the sense of kinship with men of like mind, without the occupation with the objective world, the eternally unattainable in the field of art and scientific endeavours, life would have seemed empty to me. The trite objects of human efforts—possessions, outward success, luxury—have always seemed to me contemptible."

He was a democrat at heart. He did not cherish the attention he received for his genius. He wrote, "My political ideal is democracy. Let every man be respected as an individual and no man idolized. It is an irony of fate that I myself have been the recipient of excessive admiration and reverence from my fellow-beings, through no fault, and no merit of my own. The cause of this may well be the desire, unattainable for many, to understand the few ideas to which I have with my feeble powers attained through ceaseless struggle. I am quite aware that for any organization to reach its goals, one man must do the thinking and directing and generally bear the responsibility."

His observations on human nature, man's tendency to seek power and the possibility of power leading to corruption are still very valid. "But the led (the masses) must not be coerced; they must be able to choose their leader. In my opinion, an autocratic system of coercion soon degenerates; force attracts men of low morality. The really valuable thing in the pageant of human life seems to me not the political state, but the creative, sentient individual, the personality; it alone creates the noble and the sublime, while the herd as such remains dull in thought and dull in feeling."

"This topic brings me to that worst outcrop of herd life, the military system, which I abhor. This plague-spot of civilization ought to be abolished with all possible speed. Heroism on command, senseless violence, and all the loathsome nonsense that go by the name of patriotism—how passionately I hate them!"

"The most beautiful experience we can have is the mysterious. It is the fundamental emotion that stands at the cradle of true art and true science. Whoever does not know it and can no longer wonder, no longer marvel, is as good as dead, and his eyes are dimmed. It was the experience of mystery even if mixed with fear that engendered religion. a knowledge of the existence of something we cannot penetrate, our perceptions of the profoundest reason and the most radiant beauty, which only in their most primitive forms are accessible to our minds; it is this knowledge and this emotion that constitutes true religiosity. In this sense, and only this sense, I am a deeply religious man. I am satisfied with the mystery of life's eternity and with knowledge, a sense of the marvellous structure of existence as well as the humble attempt to understand even a tiny portion of the reason that manifests itself in nature."

□